The Final Summer of Vodka

LOUISE BELL

DEDICATION

For Gucci. My best friend, confidant and soul mutt.

CONTENTS

ACKNOWLEDGMENTS

I would like to thank my single life as without that there would be no book. Special thanks to friends and ex suitors for character inspiration. Big shout out to all that love Marmaris in Turkey, to Gucci for being the love of his Mummies life and to Dan for helping to show an ex Rep how to publish a book.

April 3rd 2011

Dear Diary,

Hello. My name is Lei. I am a 30 year old British single gal living in Marmaris, Turkey. I am a vegetarian and a vodka lover.

I have not kept a diary since I was 14 years old. It ended very badly with my Mum reading it and circling all the paragraphs that she did not agree with. This was highly embarrassing for me as I had detailed every last thing that I had been getting up to with my boyfriend at the time, and she bloody well circled those bits too. #Mortified

Mum if you are reading this now then I suggest that you put this down immediately. I predict if last night was anything to go by, then this diary may give you an effing heart attack.

Anyway, I have decided to write this now as firstly my Mum does not live in the same country as me and secondly, in most single gal's lives, there comes a time when one needs to step up and keep a diary of sorts to start documenting one's shenanigans to see where I am going wrong.

With this being my final summer of vodka and all, you could say now is a good a time as any.

This summer is going to be a big deal for me. This is the summer that is going to be the end of all my single gal ways. It is to be the end of an era, a mark in my life.

This summer I am going to find the one.

Yes dear diary, I have made it my main goal and my only aim; the only thing I plan to accomplish this summer is to find my man. This is the guy that is going to sweep me off my feet, the one that I will fondly refer to as my other half, fuck it, let's be cheesy and roll with 'my mate'.

I believe that it's high time to stop all the pissing about, partying and general living of single life and get cracking with coupledom. I'm at that age where it just makes sense. I am feeling that male company on a full

3

time basis is absolutely required from here on in.

I live in hope that I will find my knight in shining armour by the end of this season. Now let me be clear here, I am not looking for some sort of tit in a tin can. No. I have had my fair share of those, in fact I have had everybody's fair share. So to be mighty specific, I am literally looking for the real deal.

Even though it comes across this way, I am not one of those girls with a time line and a baby goal. Bloody hell no. I have simply arrived at the point in my life where I know that I'm ready to meet the man that I am supposed to be with. And, by the end of the summer, come hell or high water I need to have found him.

Its official, my green light is on.

So, welcome to my world. My sometimes dark depressing world, but welcome none the less.

Let me give you somewhat of an insight about me:

My life is relatively normal. I live alone with the current love of my life Gucci Prince Michael the 2nd (My ridiculously wonderful dog - Guch for short), a car named Kastro and a scooter named Betty.

I have a great team of Mingers (terribly good friends) that I love dearly (most of the time) and a non-blood related Sister of the opposite sex. Sound pretty normal so far? I would say so. However I live in a land filled with mostly abnormal people. Firstly Marmaris is home of the Turkish love rat. I won't bore you with the stories as I'm sure you've heard many, but what Marmaris also attracts is the crazies, the self obsessed and the downright psychotic ex pats in search of a better life and cheaper beer. Sometimes this rubs off on you and you get sucked in to the pointless drama of it all, but if you are clever (and you would be wise to be so), you dust this unwelcome shit off as quickly as possible and steer clear of the unwanteds.

I was born in Manchester and being that my Mum is from South Africa, we have done quite a lot of travelling in our time. This gave me the bug. I won't go into too much detail about the how's and why's that got me living here, but I had just gotten rid of a nob head when I looked around at the grey skies and thought fuck it, I need me some sun. Don't care where, but I want that flight and I want that beach. And that's just what I did. Nothing and no one could have stopped me hopping on that plane back then. Now would be a different story entirely....

I like most, have an ex. He was the thorn in my side for a heck of a long time. When I say thorn, I obviously mean the one that got away, the one that broke my heart, the one that I should steer well clear of in all future endeavours, and the one that I always drunk text. As soon as I get close to removing his presence from my life, he for some reason starts to rear his head again. I have had to input him in my mobile as 'Do not Drunk Dial FFS', but even that doesn't work. Why don't I delete his number? Like most good ex stalkers, I know it by heart drunk or sober. So my way of thinking was to name him something that may put me off dialling. It doesn't.

I can pull my shit together when I need to as I somehow found myself running my own business. I don't quite know how that happened, but it did none the less. Well, that's a bit of a fib, I know exactly how I ended up where I am. My ex boss decided to not pay me for 3 months and rip me off all at the same time. Once this happened I decided to take a few months off to contemplate life. Vodka was the key ingredient in the contemplation process. Once the process was complete, my mind was made up. I had decided to become a show girl in Vegas. If Holly Madison can do it, then I'm sure as shit I can too. In the mean time I decided to go full throttle with the business while I work on removing my stomach.

To survive living in Marmaris I have had to pretty much work like a dog to make ends meet, everyone has to. There have been the best friendships ever formed and a million memories made (some that have been forgotten due to the vodka) and most of those memories were made whilst I worked as a holiday rep.

Don't get me wrong, it's not always wonderful living here. Sometimes the grass is not always greener. Sometimes it really pisses me off. But I'm still here and I don't feel like moving anywhere else most of the time.

So, as you can see, I am a normal(ish) kind of gal. I don't have any weird fetishes that I need to point out, nor do I have any obsessive compulsive disorders.

In all honesty my life is as bog standard as they come. It's not glamorous, it's not mundane. But you really couldn't make it up…

Chapter 1 - April 2011

8th April

Dear my rich and married self in an alternate universe,

The start of the month has been like the start of any other. I have worked to survive, I have partied like the aging rock star that I am and I have eyed up a few nice looking blokes.

At the moment I am finding great difficulty in flirting. I seem to have lost that ability and I don't know why. I want to find a bloke that sparks my interest as well as my libido but where are they all? These last couple of years I seem to have found myself stuck in a rut of meeting no one. I don't mean no hopers, I mean no one.

I am going to let the ex take full credit for this. I am going to go as far to say that the arsehole may have ruined me for life. We had a great relationship until it he was summoned to do his compulsory military service. Then he went all odd. I can't explain how, but trust me on the odd bit. I truly madly deeply loved him. I don't think I had ever been in love with anyone until him.

And that dear diary is why I am struggling.

I sometimes have horrific thoughts that I am not going to find love here in Marmaris. The resort boys with their huge gelled hair that is the size of the Eiffel Tower do absolutely nothing for me.

I want a man that has got something about him, that does not need a woman for money, that is in the same age group as me, that is adventurous and spontaneous yet organised, and most of all, that speaks my language and I don't just mean English. I need this man to get me. I need him to show me what this world is all about. I need him to totally sweep me off my feet and damn well surprise me as God knows, there aren't many surprises in my life these days.

Oh universe, please deliver me my Mr. Right soon, I'm bored of being single now...

18th April

Dear world that is testing me,

Last night I decided to stop off at a rather nice view point up in the hills of Marmaris with a young man that I met on the internet. Yes I do these random internet dating things occasionally and never once have they ended well.

The thing is I didn't even like his pictures, but I'm a trier and you never know if he may have used fugly pics of himself in case he happens to be a beautiful model that is struggling to find love because of who he is. #Nosuchluck

I had no intention of snogging the life out of him, yet I could see it was on his cards from the glint in his eye and the statement that he made: 'Your eyes are like diamonds, we are mates', and with that, my interest disappeared along with my libido, never to return again (for him anyway).

The police were doing their rounds and happened to come a knockin' at Kastro's window mentioning that my music was too loud. I had good reason for that as I had to drown out the cheese that internet boy was spouting somehow didn't I?

The police man didn't speak much English and what with my horrific Turkish (yes I know, after all these years I should be able to string a sentence together other than swear words), I didn't have a clue what he was yammering on about until I saw the big truck coming up the hill and I instantly knew that that particular truck had Kastros name all over it. Bastard!

The vile Police man went on to receive an inordinate amount of abuse from me and the young cheese suddenly seemed to have disappeared leaving me alone to deal with the crap I had gotten myself into. What a nice young cheese, NOT.

I do not recommend kicking off with Turkish police men. They are scary buggers that carry guns. It wouldn't have taken much more to tip this bugger over the edge with my mouth working the way it did. As you can see I'm clearly not dead, yet I am writing from the inside of a cell. Jokes. But it wouldn't have taken much.

As I watched Kastro on the truck going down the hill, I realized that I was rather a long way from home with not a taxi in sight. Well, I can't blame the taxi drivers; I was in the middle of nowhere, up a hill in the pitch black of night. Kind of like a horror movie, I could just imagine a mad man with a machete coming along and be-heading me at any minute.

So with no other option, I started on my long walk home. With every step I took I got angrier and angrier. None of the Mingers were answering their phones (being 2am, why would they?) so I had to grin and bear it.

Then I did something rather stupid. I text the ex. Mo Fo didn't reply.

When I eventually made it home a few hours later, I stuck my nose in the fridge and hunted for the vodka. I believe that I have never deserved vodka more. Something that usually happens after throwing a shot of vodka down my throat to sort my face out, would usually result in me sending myself off to bed. But that didn't happen. What did happen was me drinking half the bottle of vodka and Facebooking.

Seriously do I never learn? Who did I Facebook? My ex of course. He got it all that night. All that plus more the poor dear.

Eventually bed called and I passed out into an alcohol induced kip. I woke up with a stinking hangover and the Guch on my face. Great. Then as it occasionally does, some memory returned. "Fuck my Life" sprung to mind.

After sorting the mess of my head out, I got to work on sorting the mess of Kastro out.

Funnily enough, the ex text giving me some advice. Not on getting the car out of the impound like you would imagine. Oh no. The arse gave me advice about drunk Facebooking.

Thanks dick face.

Thankfully Kimmy Minger came to the rescue. Kimmy is a long-time friend/Minger of mine and I love her like a sister. We worked together as reps quite some time ago and we have never lost touch since. We are literally like chalk and cheese. Kimmy being the sensible one and me being the loose cannon. Our friendship works. Sometimes, when I spiral out of control, Kimmy brings me back onto the planet. She is the voice of reason. She too has suffered a great deal of heartbreak, and over this heartbreak is where our friendship really began. One day soon this biatch will be my maid of honour, but until then, bestie will do.

Anyway Kimmy helped out a Minger in distress and took me to the car impound, but as she had to leave for work, she could literally only drop me off at the place (that happens to be miles away from anywhere in Marmaris). I started the search for Kastro but no Kastro in sight. Why? Cos I was at the wrong sodding car impound that's why. Justmyluck.com. I found myself once again stuck in the middle of nowhere, alone, with not a soul to be seen. To make matters worse I had also ran out of credit on my phone. At least it was day light, right?

I was resigning myself to another long walk back into town when I spotted a man on a scooter. Before he could say no, I hopped on the back and made him drive off into the sunset. Unfortunately we didn't elope as fate didn't jump in. You guessed it, he was not exactly a cute guy, more rather beauty impaired, but the nice beauty impaired guy did help me out big time. He stopped me from getting eaten by wolves and he drove me to the correct place to collect Kastro. However, it is never as simple as it seems for me. I had to go to the cop shop and spend three friggin' horrific hours there pleading with them to release Kastro. Then off course they wouldn't. Why? Because this is Turkey and I am a single female without a boyfriend to help me out. The nice beauty impaired guy on the scooter had to go as obviously he has a life of his own and does not masquerade as superman for the full day, so I called upon the assistance of a rather good pal of mine instead, Kaan.

Kaan is a diamond. We fight like husband and wife but don't have the benefits of the makeup sex, so what happens is there is lots of sexual tension that builds up and up and up. Without the sweet relief of sex, we end up not speaking to each other for a couple of months or so then have a vodka night and all is well again. I like him immensely. He is clever, has a lot going for him, funny (even though I don't think he means to be) and is a good friend that doesn't judge me.

Anyway, God love him, he showed up, whizzed me around everywhere, got it all sorted and not one sarcastic word crept out of his mouth. The looks said it all though.

All hail good pals that take time out of work to help out silly British females!

And the young cheese? Not even one text to find out if everything is OK after ditching me. See, this is why I should never go near fugly internet men…

Chapter 2 - May 2011

1st May

Dear my non hung-over self in an alternate universe,

Do not drink again.

Today started off with a hangover. I really should know by now that Sunday fun day drinking is the absolute worst. On Mondays I always have far too much work to catch up on and the hangovers usually render me useless for the day. I actually hate Mondays. And today, I hate myself too.

Don't get me wrong here; I'm the next best thing since sliced bread when the party is in full swing. I'm one of these people that can't say no. I'm the last to leave a night out, a house party, a restaurant where there is alcohol, well you get the general picture. I literally want to rave all night long. I am the life and of most nights out as I'm like the Duracell bunny and can just keep going. I bloody love a good party. It always seems like such a good idea at the time. That is until now, when I have hit the deck. I have totally crashed. I am me no longer. I am now a quivering wreck holding Guch hostage as I need cuddles and water to not die in the corner on my cold kitchen floor. But I need to be on this cold kitchen floor as when I head back to the sofa I get hot sweats, so staying here is the best place for me right now.

My weekend was a messy one. It involved much ex texting and humiliation.

In fact I am that ashamed of myself that I don't wish to document it, however this is my diary after all and I suppose if I document it, it may shame me into never doing it again.

Friday was a night at home. Good girl. I didn't drink a drop. Saturday was different. I had a beer in the afternoon at home whilst sitting on the balcony contemplating life. I was alone other than Guch for company. My one beer turned into three as it was very nice out on the balcony. Three beers is a bugger of a number as it urged me to text that shit of an ex. Now I didn't feel like playing nice with him, so I basically did my usual 'How very dare you' text and immediately got a reply asking if he could come over. Three beers agreed to him coming over on the understanding that he brings with him more beer. He was at my door 30 minutes later with many more beers. We were having a grand old time chit chatting and getting through the beers like no tomorrow and before I knew it, it was dark and gone 11pm. He seemed like he wanted to get something off his chest. I could just tell he was itching to discuss something.

He went on to make an odd statement, he told me he missed the old me. I could feel anger brewing within me. I tried to remain calm when I told him that the present hard faced cow is what he created. He didn't quite understand, so I went on to explain to him that I am now not the nice sweet gal that he used to adore due to *his* behaviour and how *he* has dicked me around. The old me has died, gone up in a blaze of glory, and the new more slender me is what's been left in its place. I think he got it. But then he asked me to revert back as the older chubbier version was nicer. Rage was coming to the surface once again. I took the glass of beer out of his hand and threw it at him. I quite literally had a mental breakdown. I demanded that he leave immediately whilst screaming and shouting like a crazed lunatic. He did in fact leave immediately.

I then text giving more abuse and calling him a total twat for leaving and not being able to take the truth, demanding that he come back. I got one reply to 7 messages and that was informing me that he won't be speaking to me again. Oh here's fucking hoping fuck face! Don't like the monster you have made no? Well fuck off then and let the monster find someone new to abuse instead then.

I guarantee that the sap will speak to me again. His promises aint worth shit unfortunately. In all honesty, I need him not to speak to me and follow it through. Maybe then I will have a cat in hell's chance at getting over this mo fo. Alas, I know what will happen. It may go two weeks to a month, I will text him and he will reply. It's a vicious circle. The day he gets married is the day I know that he will finally be off the table. I won't like it much, but at least it will put an end to all this 'is he or isn't he' getting back with me ridiculousness.

I actually hate him right now. But then I want him at the same time. They say you always want what you can't have. If I could have him so easily I probably wouldn't want him anymore. Why can't you help me out here universe, put me out of my misery and throw me a bone. Let that fucker come crawling so I can get on with my damn life.

So, that was Saturday …

Sunday arrived with impending doom. A normal occurrence these days. Nothing else for it but to indulge in Sunday fun day with Team Minger. I can tell you I was home in bed by 12am, and I can tell you that Jess and I were nearly at fisticuffs as she wrestled me to the ground trying to remove the phone out of my hand whilst I was in a desperate attempt to text shit ex.

Jess the Minger is like my older sister. She knows that nothing good will come of texting that twat of an ex. I also believe that Jess may have a liver of steel. She moved over here 4 years ago with her daughter Saffy (who we lovingly call 'the Minglett'). We were not always friends let me tell you. In fact at first we really didn't like each other. It was her Mum that was my friend. Sadly she passed away, but, since then, Jess the Minger and I seem to have found that neither one of us is as truly vile as we originally thought.

Anyway, back to the at hand: Jess won the phone fight and I sent myself home in a strop. With no phone there was nothing else left to do other than turn on the trusty lap top and Facebook message him instead. We are not friends on Facebook so I couldn't tell if he was online or not, but he got a few nasty messages, and then I sent myself up to bed with a flea in my ear.

Which brings us up to today, where I am writing to you from the cold and bloody uncomfortable kitchen floor. The ex has not replied to my torrent of Facebook abuse, I am filled with alcohol depression and self loathing and I think I am going to be single for eternity. At least Guch loves me. God I do not know where I would be without him.

And with that, it's time to call it a night, send myself up to bed to watch a bit of Lost and hope that tomorrow will be brighter.

Fuck you life. Fuck you.

3rd May

Dear self that does not listen,

Do not drink again. Seriously this time.

I had better explain…

After a hard day at work, I went to see some friend's performing in their new drag show. It was the opening night so all and sundry had been invited. It was very busy indeed with everyone wanting to catch a glimpse of the famous willies in fillies, so when Team Minger were seated in the VIP section for no apparent reason, lots of glares and 'who do they think they are' comments were flying around the room. Ex Pats in Marmaris are neither gracious nor quiet speakers...

I had gone out with the intention of not drinking. In fact all the Mingers were officially 'off it' for the night, but alas, as all Mingers know, it's just plain rude not to have a little vodka whilst socialising, and I will never be one of those rude girls that go upsetting folk due to not wanting to indulge in a little vodka. That's when it happened. That's when I saw '*her*', my ex-friend. I say ex-friend as the slut bag dated my ex-boyfriend right after me.

Jan and I were not friends when the ex and I were together, but when he went to the army to do his military service for 15 months, we became friends through the winter period. I told her everything. She gave me a fresh pair of ears to listen to my many thousand issues of the ex wanting to get back with me then dumping me time and time again… We basically came to the conclusion, that he was being a dick as he was in the army with no control over anything and couldn't stand it if I cheated on him whilst he was in there. I had no intention of cheating as he was the love of my life. He was the one and she damn well knew it.

When he came out of the army, we started up again, on and off. He was stringing me along and any fool could see it except this fool. I thought that if I just gave him time he would become the guy that I had fallen for once again.

Instead he started dating her. Fucking Jan.

So, I naturally indulged in a vodka or 8 with those very same Mingers that were officially 'off it' and my good pal Kaan. It helped. Notice how I don't call Kaan a Minger? That's because he simply is not. He is a rather well respected business man, but to me, he is just my buddy. Anyway, more about him later.

As vodka would have it, we all got good and drunk. Thankfully I managed to dodge Jan, and luckily she left the show early. That could have been something to do with Team Minger giving her the evils and the occasional middle finger, but I could be wrong. I am really unsure as to what would have happened if we were in the same three square feet, say the toilet, whilst intoxicated. I'm glad I didn't have the chance to find out. One day I will, but the time is not now.

After the show was over we ended up going to another bar where I bumped into my pal (the owner) and also his pal (another friend of mine and the owner of another bar), confusing I know. They were clearly ever so slightly intoxicated but always good fun so I thought; 'another vodka it is then'!

Jess was not feeling the love for that particular bar, and when Jess aint feeling the love, it means it's time to go. Although Jess is one of my closest friends here, she does tend to want to do things her way and her way alone. When she's got a bee in her vodka, there is no point in arguing with her. That being said, she has a heart of gold and generally would always be there for me when I need her.

Jess really did not want to be at the bar, so the boys suggested walking her to the taxi rank and then coming back to party. That idea suited me down to the ground as all Jess was doing was moaning that she wasn't getting any free drinks. Mingers eh... Whilst walking, she made a rather good point (she makes these occasionally), she said that being slightly intoxicated myself I may not have noticed that the boys were looking at me like a piece of meat that was about to get flung on the barbecue. Well knock me down with a feather! I bloody well did not wish to get flung on the barby so that put paid to me going back to the bar. I cleverly went home and abused Facebook instead. Good work clever girl, good work.

8th May

Dear girl that will never learn,

Saturday is a great day for me. I truly love a Saturday through and through. The day starts with the omnibus of Eastenders. I am one of these crazy characters that choose to not watch Eastenders nightly. I like to save mine up all in one to watch on my favourite day. Once the 'benders from Eastenders' is over, it's time to decide what the crack is going to be for the evening. Saturday night is THE night out of the week so you guessed it, I absolutely had to go out.

I don't really remember much of Saturday evening. This is quite normal. If I drink 3 Vodka's or 13, the result is always the same: memory loss. I know I went out and I know I woke up with a hangover. Yes I suffered. But I can truly say that it was worth it (I think). Team Minger hit Cheers and then Bar Street, then back to Jess the Mingers house for some more partying until 7am. Another normal night out. The photos are horrific and that nasty cow Jess tagged me in every single one.

You will be happy to hear that I did not partake in any texting of the ex. In fact it was a no man night all together, we were all just so happy to have each other that we did not require male company. Don't ya just love those kind of nights?

To dull the pain of my Sunday hangover, I took my suffering self down to the beach front and had a shandy or two.

Random shandy induced thought: 'Boyfriend Interviews'– Hmm interesting. Must remember this for future reference.

12th May

Dear silly flirty girl,

It has been a sodding stressful week at work let me tell you. When I get over stressed I like to have a little drink, so I held an impromptu vodka night at my house with Kaan. This is quite a regular occurrence. For some reason when Kaan and I have Vodka night, we never wish to invite anyone else. I guess it's a bit of a private thing, especially with all that pent up sexual tension going on that we pretend doesn't exist. Since we met, there has always been this weird underlying flirtation. We have never crossed the line and I never believed that we would. But what you believe and what actually happens are two different things.

Fuelled with vodka, something rather odd happened. We ended up snogging on the sofa like a pair of mentally disturbed teenagers filled with angst.

The funny thing about it was that I quite liked it.

What is it they say, don't shit where you eat? This cannot end well.

15th May

Dear wannabe socialite that always attracts the wrong kind of bloke,

This weekend was a bit of an odd one. I had no time to wonder where snogging my best guy pal came from as I had an internet man flying down to visit me from Istanbul. WTF Right? It's not the first time he has been to see me, so I knew what I was letting myself in for. Thankfully he is ruggedly handsome, tall, speaks perfect English and rather rich – what more could a gal ask for? Well, the cherry is that he has got the most amazingly stinking attitude ever known to man. Why did I have him here when I knew what I letting myself in for? Well, the last time he was here was 2 and a half years ago and I thought he may have changed. Boy was I ever wrong. He has never once enquired as to what my line of work happens to be. So whilst having lunch I asked him if he was ever going to ask me what I did for a living. His reply was what I should have expected, however I could not keep the horrified look from creeping across my face when he said 'I just don't give a shit'. When I asked why, he summed it up in one: 'I am just not interested unless it involves me'. Well that told me didn't it.

I am surprised that I didn't turn into the arse kicking ninja that I usually would and get rid of Mr. Attitude immediately, however, as he was only here for the weekend (and the sex was not too bad) I decided to hell with his stinking attitude and I let him pay for everything like any normal single wannabe socialite would.

He has however once more reminded me why I do not wish to see him. He is OK for a lost weekend, but is it even worth that?

Mental note for the future: You do not wish to invite him over again until all the men in Marmaris have left the building.

Dick.

Me I mean.

17th May

Dear stupid stalker within,

A full week has now passed since my random snogging session with Kaan. Do I feel weird about it? Yes and no, but due to Mr. Attitude being here it took the onus off that situation. That was until now.

Sister and I had made plans to go out and have a couple of sociable drinks. Sister does not go out and do that much these days, I think he may be feeling his age. He never used to be like this. I remember the days when Sister and I would sit up all night ploughing our way through 7 bottles of wine just for the sake of it on long boring winter nights in Marmaris. You see when one Sister starts, the other usually follows. We were living together at the time and had not much else to do, so why not eh?

I have known Sister for a terribly long time, I would say about 10 years now. We used to work together as lowly reps (as previously mentioned, most of my favourite people in the world were met while repping). Sister truly is one of a kind. He is a 45 year old gay man that is so laid back he is actually aging backwards. That could be down to the Botox, but whatever floats your boat. The guy never worries about anything. Seriously, never. He does need a boot up the backside to do absolutely everything and being that I am one of these super organized freaks that needs things done quickly and in a certain way, I do have the tendency to flip out about silly crap when dear Sister remains calm. He lets me have my hissy fit and then continues to do whatever laid back thing he was doing prior to said hissy fit. Yes it's safe to say, I love my dear Sister, but he doesn't half wind me up at times.

Anyway, as I was saying, we were planning on going to see yet another drag show (drag is literally the only thing available in Marmaris). I asked Kaan if he would like to join us. He turned me down for the show, but we met up later on in Cheers. I can't say that it was a weird because it wasn't. However when looking at him, the stomach started doing odd things that it had never done before. I willed it to be the dodgy omelette I had for dinner, however willing something doesn't mean that it will just go away does it? The feelings just wouldn't take the hint. I needed to subside these silly feelings and immediately! I mean what if he could see right through me and know what was going on in my mind? Vodka was the answer. Lots of Vodka. Maybe too much sodding vodka as when Kaan left, what did I do? I got my phone out and texted him, that's what I did. Nothing too bad, however when I didn't get a reply within 2 minutes, I text again and then again – sending a total of 8 texts. All of which went unanswered.

How much of a pathetic loser am I? Well, in answer to that question – this is how much: when arriving home, feeling rather sorry for myself, I text the ex. Yet another unanswered text. With that really topping off my self esteem, I took Gucci to bed with me to perve over Link Burrows in Prison Break.

God I really am a tit. And a bit of a sad act too.

18th May

Dear my disillusioned self,

I woke up with the beeping of my phone. Oh yey – someone has finally text me back! Looser alert, it was only Turkcell, my bestest friend in the world right now sending me some crap offer. But I did notice a text that I hadn't heard coming through. It was from Kaan wishing me a good morning! Joy of Joys I am not such a sad pathetic looser after all! Or am I? Well the answer is a plain and simple yes indeed I am; however not right now as he has just invited me out to lunch. Crap, what to wear? I opted for a rather casual look of black combats, black vest top and trilby. I believe that apart from the birds nest on my head (that was ever so brilliantly covered by the trilby), I looked half human. Good job.

Lunch was good, however I was not expecting to discuss the snogging. Seriously, that one came as a shock, so the only thing to do was pull a shaggy on his arse and go with 'it wasn't me'.

All the Mingers know that when I drink, I tend to lose a lot of memory. So yes, it was maybe not the best thing to do, but being caught off guard and in somewhat of a state of shock, I opted for no recollection of it ever happening. It worked ☺

So the snogging was mentioned, a lot of underlying flirting was also going on and my stomach was doing back flips again.

After the 2 hour lunch, we came to the decision that maybe having vodka night at my house was not the best of ideas. I tried to argue that we had had it there many a time before yet had not had a snogging incident, but reality bites and not having vodka night at home was probably for the best.

I came home and mulled over my eventful lunch and decided to text Kaan asking for a vodka night. Jesus Lei, sort your shit out girl! I should actually take this advice however the reply I got from Kaan was positive – he said, and I quote "we can't kiss in Cheers so best to have it at home☺". I laughed for about 20 minutes before feeling all girly and downright happy about this rather odd situation. We have planned the home vodka night for possibly tomorrow night.

I think I may have swallowed a bag of crack as this is not something that I should be getting into with this wonderful friend of mine. I mean for the love of god, have all the males in Marmaris disappeared or something leaving me to only have my best male non gay friend as an option? I need to sort my head out seriously, but not right now as I have vodka night to plan.

Do I want to have another snogging session? I shouldn't but I do.

Nothing good can ever come from this.

And then the ex finally replied, a whole day later. I knew that fucker couldn't keep his promise of never speaking to me again. I can read that tit like a book. He mentioned that I probably didn't remember sending him a message last night, and how I should think about staying home a bit more instead of always partying. Well, he can just piss off with his judgmental ways insinuating that I was intoxicated.

Loser.

Once again, I mean me.

19th May

Dear the normal girl that lurks somewhere deep within,

I have sorted my head out since yesterday and I most certainly do not wish
to have another snogging session on the sofa with my dear friend Kaan
who happens to be coming over tonight. I would rather keep a good friend
than go down that road as I am absolutely certain that we could not
continue to be friends if anything was to happen. I tend to bunny boil and
over obsess about these situations (actually any situation), and I just do not
like myself when I do these things. Normally I am pretty much out spoken
but cool – however when I over obsess its 'psycho alert'! At least I know
this about myself and can stop anything before it really gets started. So it's
a good thing right?

With Kaan due in less than half an hour, I best start sprucing myself up, get
the candles out and the music on. Hang on – stop – take stock. WTF am I
doing? I don't want another snogging session so best change that plan of
action to full bright lights, normal TV on in background and I best Minger
myself up by picking a few spots so they are big and red for when he
arrives.

Oh fuck me; this is going to be fun…

20th May

Dear fool that lurks on the boarder,

Kaan came over, we drank, we talked, we really really talked, and he left with no snogging in sight.

Am I proud of myself? Oh yes. Am I annoyed? Oh yes! I know I had my mind made up re the snogging, however it wouldn't have been a completely horrific experience to have had a little snog. I am up and down like a frikkin' yo-yo at the moment. One day I am totally against the snogging and the next I want it like I have never wanted anything before in my life. You may ask why is it I am so against the snogging as clearly Kaan and I get on so well? Did I forget to mention that Kaan is already spoken for? Reason numero uno for not going anywhere near him in future… But sometimes I do believe that we are star crossed lovers.

Note to self: Kaan is your friend but he is also someone else's man. You are a wanker and should not fancy someone else's man. Stop.

He asked me last night that if he was not seeing someone, would I date him? Inside I was screaming OH YES, but what came out of my mouth was a bit different. I am not one that easily shows my feelings you see, however writing about them is of no issue what so ever. So what did come out of my mouth? "Urm, maybe, maybe not, but you're a bit tall and not really my type as you have dark circles around your eyes and resemble lurch".

Classy – real classy.

24ᵗʰ May

Dear happy self,

I have had a rather manic few days to say the least. Sometimes it's not all bad you know, this living thing that we do…

Let me begin with Saturday night's antics: To start the night off, I went to visit Jess the Minger at the hotel where she works. I decided to indulge in a few vodkas as it is my last summer of vodka after all. I slightly lost track of time as Emre, one of my coolest gay pals had text asking me where the hell I was – I should have met up with him 15 minutes earlier however the vodka was telling me otherwise.

Emre is one of these people that I have known for years. Sometimes we see each other, sometimes we don't. We don't take offence when the other is too busy and has not been in contact. He is a Turkish rep and was married. He has finally come out of the closet and is as gay as they come. I like Emre immensely as he is just so much fun. He really does not give a crap about what other people say or think about him. To sum it up, he is my kind of guy.

Anyway I headed on over to meet him plus Kimmy Minger and set about hitting the Cosmo's. After consuming enough alcohol to have powered a village for three years we headed down to bar street. That's where I met a man. Yes you heard me right – I met a man! He's not spoken for, not bad looking, spoke not too bad English and what really impressed me was his line of business – he teaches the law of attraction, well NLP anyway. Did I mention that I have an obsession with this sort of stuff, the universe and such? OMFG – This could be my mate, you know, the one that I have been waiting for! It could also be something else, it could be nothing at all, as let's face it with my track record what could I really hope for? Anyway, this cute guy (that was invited by Emre), suddenly shows up out of nowhere! Well not really out of nowhere, Emre did mention he was coming but told me nothing about him other than he thought he wouldn't be my type. I have made allowances for worse…

The night continued and I had more drinks thrust in my hand (due to me ordering them from the waiter), and I got slightly tipsy. That could be a slight understatement to be fair. The cute NLP guy took me to his office which I must say impressed me very much. Why the hell did I go to his office whilst rather intoxicated? Well, he asked, and it seemed like a good idea at the time – doesn't it always? Nothing happened in the office by the way. Dam him and his gentlemanliness. But I did get his digits ☺

After leaving I decided to call upon Jess to see if she was still awake and luckily for me she was. Why wouldn't she be at 05.30am? As always she was not surprised to see me as it's a regular occurrence for me to come a knockin' at that time. We continued to intoxicate ourselves, danced, annoyed the hell out of her boyfriend and pissed about with the dog. By 8am I had had my fill and took myself home for a well deserved crash.

Waking up on a Sunday is never a pleasant experience. Once again I had forgotten to bring the water and alka seltzer up to bed with me. Damn my stupidity! It didn't help that Gucci was desperate for a wee and decided to do it up the wall. Damn that wee infested dog!

When I finally peeled the top lid from the bottom, I noticed that I had got a text from the NLP guy! Yes indeed I had! But it only had his name on it. How odd. Maybe it was to remind me that I had met him?

Anyway, I went about my day as best as I could with a stinker of a hangover. I needed to pull myself together as it was BBQ night at Jess's hotel and I was desperate to fill my hung-over face. Which I did by the way. I also managed to behave and only consumed 2 shandies. How very British of me.

Monday and Tuesday arrived and disappeared in a flash. I have been rather busy with work and haven't had much time to party thank god, however I know that is about to change as my friend Vicky arrived in town today, so guess who I'm meeting up with very soon?

I have known Vicky since arriving in Turkey back in 1997 and she is a wicked assed woman to party with. We manage to get ourselves in the most ridiculous of situations; however I shall save those stories for another time.

Enough of that for now, time to smoke the last fag in the packet and call it a night.

P.S - I got rudely awoken last night at 03.30am to the annoying ring of my phone. Guess who had the nerve to call me? That horrific young cheese! I cancelled the call, but that didn't deter that little fucker. Oh No! He continued to harass me with ridiculous texts asking me if I wanted to drink, which in turn gave me terrible nightmares of him breaking into my house and drinking all my vodka.

P.P.S – I have not participated in any stalking of the ex or of Kaan this week.

Bravo me!

27ᵗʰ May

Dear my single self,

I went and got my cards read last night with my friend Lorraine. I met Lorraine about 6 years ago and we just sort of clicked. As we know each other so terribly well, it is more like she is my Auntie than just a friend, and with all Aunties, they can be overbearing at times. What do they say, familiarity breeds contempt? As much as we love each other, we sometimes don't like each other very much.

She is into Angel Cards and that sort of thing too, so what with me being super obsessed with wanting to learn the future, it's great that I have Lorraine to indulge in my obsession with me.

I had an alright reading, but I didn't hear the news that I had hoped for. Mr. Right is not on his way yet – but I was suitably impressed with apparently having 3 suitors in the wings just waiting for me to look their way. Apparently I'm to just get on with Mr. Right Now for the time being. Well, what Fiona the card lady actually said was that Mr. Right would not come a knockin' until I write a book… But who the hell would want to read a book written by me? I can't think of anything more horrific!

Is the NLP guy making the cut in the cards I wonder? Damn him actually as I have not even heard a dickey bird out of him recently…

My reading also mentioned that I am to be seen in front of the camera. It's no secret that I am desperate to make it to the big time. Here or anywhere, but preferably here. Other cards told me to be persistent and start getting in touch with publishers. I interpreted this to mean getting in touch with TV production companies. So I did. My goal is to land myself a reality show – honest to god, it would be great as you just couldn't make my life up.

This morning I had an email from a production company asking me to send in my 'script'. Didn't have a script, so that puts paid to that then. Well, for now anyway.

29th May

Dear sad loser that stays home on a Saturday night,

I didn't go out last night. Shock, horror! I know, what the hell is wrong with me? I went to the hairdressers yesterday to get the 'oh so minging' roots done. With newly done roots I thought that would be my motivation to go out, but I had no will or patience to put on a full face of slap or even to shower my filthy self. Not like me I know.

There was a seriously good looking hairdresser in there and he caught me perving at him three times. I'm a shy kind of girl when sober and had a mega hot blush going a nasty deep shade of crimson, so I'm sure I left a shit impression, especially as I had not an ounce of makeup on, not even my mascara.

Anyway, as I was in the hairdressers for such a long arsed time that I got bored. Not even the fit hairdresser could entertain me. I ended up texting the NLP guy. He text right back asking if I wanted to meet up after he had finished his classes. I was rather up for it but there was no way I was going to leave the hairdressers in time to go home, shower, slap on some slap and find an appropriate outfit in time for 8pm. It was 7.15pm that he asked. It would have been a struggle even if I was at home. As it turned out I came home leaving the hairdressers at 9pm. 5 hours to do roots, are they frikkin' serious! That will be the last time I go there... These hairdresser's would rather piss about than get on with the job at hand. At least I had one to perv over to kill at least some of the time.

I truly embraced my Saturday night at home by stuffing my face with junk food laced in calorific beauty (after all I could afford to do so due to not going out and drinking lots of calorific beer) and then I took my self pitying butt to bed for an early night. Was I allowed to sleep? No. Firstly Vicky was on the blower asking where the hell I was, then NLP dude text again and said his early night was cut short as his friends had showed up. Then that arse from Istanbul, Mr. Attitude insisted upon ringing and ringing and ringing at 01.00am. Normally this would have been OK as people know that I go out on a Saturday night, but when you decide to have a night home for a change, it's irritating to say the least… Some people have no time boundaries (but great big brass balls).

Mr. Attitude got a mouth full today. Hopefully he will now take the hint and just piss off.

I am due to be heading over to see Jess at the hotel soon as I'm sure that she needs to stick her head in a bucket of vodka and remain there until the morning. It is the anniversary of her Mum's passing away two years ago today. Everyone knew Jess's Mum and she was just like us when it came to having a drink. We always knew her by the nick name 'halfie halfie' as it was always half a glass of vodka and half a glass of coke. We obviously have to carry this tradition on in her name.

So that's the plan for today anyway. Must choose the outfit wisely due to meeting Jess at around 6pm (pretty early doors for a party outfit), so thinking ahead is always required…

30th May

Dear paranoia,

The ex called me last night at 01.12am. I was dead to the world so only saw the missed call this morning. Now I wonder what on earth could have been on his mind at that time?

Other than the above, I had a bit of a scare last night. I thought I was pregnant so I came home early. My reasons for thinking this are as follows:

- Constantly tired and not through partying
- Dirty big spots all over the face
- Having problems trying to get a beer down me

I took a test today and thank the good lord above I am not! That Mr. Attitude would have had a fright wouldn't he! I would have told my Mother that it would have been by Immaculate Conception as I can't let her know that I actually do have sex. Although for the amount of times that I do it these days, I could be considered the new age Virgin Mary. It's just not on actually (not the fact that I am indeed not up the duff, the fact that I am near enough a new age Virgin Mary). It's not like I don't want to do it – for the love of God, I do, I really do! But as time has gone by I just don't seem to fancy anyone enough. Lorraine says that men just can't handle me. I agree that I am a strong willed bit of a handful type of gal, but I thought men enjoyed a challenge? Not in Turkey obviously.

I was even thinking of leaving the country to land a man, possibly South Africa. They are fit surfer dude types there that can maybe handle a gal like me a bit better than these Turks.

I always thought that by the time I arrived at this silly age of thirty that I would have settled down, had a ring on my finger, if not married by now. It's not happened the way I thought it would and that's depressing.

I was engaged once to an English bloke that I could have hacked to death by the end of our rather ludicrous relationship. Of course to start off with it was an OK experience, but then it wasn't. So that was the end of that. Then came the ex. Well he just about ruined me for all eternity as since we split up I have remained single for the last three years. Of course I have had some 'luck' in-between (I am not a nun after all) but as for love – no such luck yet. I have not actually given up hope that love will eventually dig me out of my single pit, but it is starting to get a bit boring this 'last single girl in Marmaris' thing.

So the cogs of the mind returned to wondering why that arse of an ex even called considering everything that has gone down with us recently. Maybe he just wanted a bit of nookie. Well he can fuck right off if he thinks he is going to get that from me. If he honestly thinks of me as a bloody booty call then colour me horrified. I may be a bitch, but I'm nobody's booty call…

I decided to text the NLP guy to take my mind off the situation, and also in the hopes that he may ask me out to dinner tomorrow night. He replied, but he didn't ask me to dinner. He is a rather shy kinda guy so he may need a bit of a shove, however I am getting bored of doing the shoving, so time to call that one a day until he grows a pair.

I was even contemplating calling Kaan and having an impromptu vodka night, but for some odd reason I just don't want to. Instead I decided to have a look on the Badoo dating website. I turned the cam on only to have 4 willies thrust in my unsuspecting face, so I turned it off again.

Decision made - I shall stick to the original Monday night plan. 'Made in Chelsea' then bed. I may have a beer though whilst considering my next plan of action in the love department.

10.15pm:

With beer now in hand, I shall return to a random thought that I had one random Sunday – Boyfriend Interviews. Could it work? I doubt it. I could sit here pondering this all night, but without putting this rather ridiculous plan into action, I will never know. I could pop my 'BF Interview' on Facebook as public and see what happens. If all else fails by the time I turn 31 in August, if still without a man of interest, this plan is getting thrust into action whether I feel like a fool or not.

OK deal made with self. Done and dusted. Now shall I just send my ex a quick text?

Chapter 3 – June 2011

1st June

Dear Hangover Wednesday,

There is a lot to be said about partying on a school night, but none of it good. I have to stop letting people influence me so easily to go out and have 'Minging Tuesday'.

What everyone says is true about hangovers lasting longer once you hit 30. I am now a sufferer of the dreaded two day hangover and although it really vexes me to endure this gulf of vileness, I still will not leave the vodka alone. Oh no, this here chump just wants to fill my boots to make sure I am not suffering for a mere three drinks.

The reason for the vile hangover is because I finally managed to hit the town with the legend that is Vicky and my lord, did we go for it! As with most nights out on the beachfront, it ended with a nasty twist. A vicious drunk queen picked a fight with me for no reason at all. I must admit my hair was not looking its best, in fact I looked like I had been dragged through a hedge backwards but there was no need to point it out and embarrass me in front of the whole group. Don't you just hate nasty drunk bitchy queens?

As nobody caught my eye, and to make matters worse, I did a fair amount of texting the ex. I really need to learn to leave my phone at home. I'm like a woman with a huge big stick that keeps prodding the bear until I get the desired response. What that may be I really don't know, but I clearly haven't got it yet as I still keep prodding. On a plus note, I literally do not have any shame any more when it comes to texting that fucker. After what he did to me, he deserves all the shit I dish out.

Now suitably embarrassed by the bitchy queen, plus my boozy impending doom, I could actually just go and sit in a dark room with nothing but Celine Dion playing and a razor blade to keep me company. OK maybe a bit overdramatic there, but you get the point.

And still not a word from the NLP dude! Sometimes life really does suck. But at least I didn't drunk text stalk him, so there is a silver lining after all. I can get away with it with the ex as he expects it, but I would be mortified if I started bunny boiling the NLP guy so soon.

I did actually try to cure the hangover by forcing Sister into coming to Dominoes with me. Not much forcing had to be done when I told him it was 2 for 1 on Pizzas. He wasn't excited at the prospect that he could save money, nope – he was excited of the prospect that he could get 2 large assed Pizzas for the price of one. And he guzzled them both in front of me knowing that I am on a serious diet. I am never one to order a salad when I eat out as it is just a waste of money, so even though I am on my diet, I ordered the 2 Pizzas, ate one shoved the other in the freezer. Clever girl. It was in the freezer for all of 20 minutes before I got it out, warmed it up and ate the whole sodding thing. Not so clever girl as it didn't help one little bit and actually made me feel sick, bloated and a like bloody big loser.

I won't dare to say that I am never drinking again as that would be a blatant lie but hangover Wednesday you are no longer welcome so please do us all a favour and piss off.

3rd June

Dear normal me,

TFI Friday! Thank god it's finally here. My period has arrived and how lovely, it's brought with it even more spots, mood swings and a ridiculously stinking attitude.

During my hangover/period/spotty phase Camilla the oldest Minger in the world gave me a rather grand idea. She has them from time to time. She is one of my oldest friends here in Marmaris and I am so glad of her even though we don't see each other too often. She has the most excellent life experience known to man, but given her age, so she should! Camilla is a 68 year old rep (I kid you not) that puts the young ones to shame. For her 60th birthday I bought her a push bike cos that's just how she roll's (pun intended ha!). I've know her now for about 10 years and we were always the naughty reps that no one wanted to manage. Camilla is probably one of the most colourful people I have ever met and I am just happy to have her around, naughtiness and all.

Anyway, the idea that she so cleverly gave me was to create a website and post some of this very diary on there as a blog. Even when I am hung-over I get rather creative and as I have put this idea into action, it has taken shape nicely and I, yes me, now have my very own blog thingy. It's an online diary of sorts, and Mum just stop reading now.

No text back from the ex after my drunk stalking thank god. Even if he had of replied, I would have pulled the usual 'It wasn't me' or 'I don't have any recollection of doing that' and that usually is enough to convince me that I am not a mentally disturbed stalker. Deep within, I'm sure my sub conscious knows that I am, but not so much of the mental more of the tipsy.

Why does vodka make me do such things? I wouldn't dream of doing it in normal coherent hours of the day (usually), so why do it when vodka has passed the lips? I knew there was a reason for this being my final summer of it.

4th June

Dear ashamed single,

Yes I am single on a Saturday night. I have just woken up after a little nap on the sofa and realized that it's Saturday night and I am all alone with nowhere to go. This makes two Saturdays in a row. What seems to be happening here? Well the Mingers are out of action, Sister has a work doo, Vicky is out with someone I dislike and Lorraine is going on a date. So that leaves me and Gucci alone again. I do not like this one little bit. I don't feel like having a drink alone as it just depresses me, but seriously, is it going to be pizza and DVD again? It definitely seems so unless my knight in shining armour / tit in the tin can finally gets the balls to ask me out on a date. #Iseriouslydoubtit as I have been waiting 2 weeks already for NLP dude to ask and still he has not.

What if this new Saturday night syndrome continues next week and then maybe the week after? O dear god, I may be doomed. I can't fathom to imagine what people will think with not seeing me out week after shocking week. Has the way I roll just changed? I suppose I could resort to going out on my own to a bar. Actually scrap that, it would be worse than staying in! People would look at me and point and stare, mutter under their breaths at the sight of me out alone. I would give the unwanteds feeding fodder for months if I did that.

So, I have resigned myself to staying home again tonight.

On the plus side, my new blog has now gone live. It's looking rather good if I do say so myself. Maybe I will sit in, get a glass of vino and just blog the hell out of blogging. Drunk blogging could become my thing, my niche, what I'm know for. Ha, I would re-read it in the morning and end up deleting the website entirely knowing my mouth when I have had a tipple!

Boring idea for the night: I should start writing a book of 101 boring ideas to do when dateless on a Saturday night. Would be a best seller wouldn't it? (To losers like me that are dateless on a Saturday night).

The boyfriend interviews seem to be looking better and better right now. Hmm, that could be an idea to pop onto my new blog thing. Or maybe not if I wish to keep an ounce of decorum. But I do want the boyfriend so I seem to be stuck between that sodding rock and hard place again.

Maybe I should grow a pair and go out alone and see what happens. I mean it's not as if I will die or anything right? Maybe I should hire an 'assistant' come single friend, then I would never have to even consider having to go out alone again. A hot sexy tight arsed assistant would fit the bill just nicely. Someone like Jake Gyllenhaal. God I love him. Michael J Fox was bloody cute too in the day with his floppy hair and his Back to the Future grin. I don't like to imagine him now with Parkinsons, that's just sad.

Why oh why am I seriously the only single gal here in Marmaris. This is not a great place to be when single and desperate to go out!

Damn you singledom, you really have me up a height tonight.

5th June

Dear saddo self,

The "non hangover" Sunday.

I woke up in a bit of a crap mood. Must be as I am used to waking with a hangover and the Guch on my face on a Sunday. I only had the Guch face sitting experience to roll with this morning, but 1 out of 2 isn't that bad. Oh well, no use crying over spilt milk, what's done is done. So what if I stayed home two Saturday nights in a row. I may make the decision right here, right now that I will not go out next Saturday, then at least it's my own decision, not one that has been taken away from me. Who the hell cares anyway if I go out or not apart from Guch (who would rather have his Mum at home with him anyway)?!

Christ, listen to me, the voice of misery! The sad Bridget Jones of bloody Marmaris. What a load of self pitying crap.

I have actually had quite a nice day. Lorraine and I went out on a long assed walk and I got to hear all about her date last night. Just kill me now please. Am I jealous that my friend had a date and I didn't? Maybe, but I covered it well with lots of 'Ooooooos and Ahhhhhssss' in all the right places while inwardly my green eyed monster was tearing her hair out.

I also took the bull by the horns today and asked the NLP dude out for drinks tomorrow night. I must admit I am not liking having to invite myself for drinks, however if I want to go for drinks with this guy then I had to make the first move. He agreed (as I hoped he would) but I would much rather not have been the one doing the asking if you know what I mean. Don't get me wrong, I am a 21st century new aged independent woman, times have changed since men were expected to do the asking, so why shouldn't I have asked him out? No big deal right? Who the hell am I trying to kid - Yes it is a bloody big deal, I should not have had to do the asking, he should have asked me and what the hell am I going to wear?

I have no idea if we are doing the dinner thing or just drinks???!!! He wants to meet in a restaurant at around 9pm so that suggests to me dinner and drinks but oh me oh my, that is just too much pressure on this single gal! I don't think I can handle this situation that I have created like a dignified classy lady, so I will just have to handle it like myself then. I may have to indulge in a shot or two of vodka before I leave the house to give me some Dutch courage and hopefully a few conversation starters too, as being the shy kinda guy that he is, I think I may need them.

Wish me luck! Or at least keep your fingers crossed that I don't pass out in a vodka induced coma before I actually leave the house to go on my date!

7th June

Dear girl that dates,

I went on the date. Can't say it was a good one, but here goes: The night started off in a random sort of way as when I opened the fridge to get my usual glass of getting ready vodka, there was no vodka in sight. Panic literally flooded through my veins when I realized I would have to arrive sober. Not a good feeling let me tell you considering I hadn't been on a date in like, forever. I was nervous as all hell and my mind started working overtime – should I go to the shop and grab a bottle? No, that was just silliness. So I used my noggin and got ready in record time and hot footed it down to Jess Minger's hotel where there is never a short supply of vodka. I managed to knock three large ones down me before heading over to meet my date.

As I chose the venue, I knew it was going to be spectacular. It overlooks the whole bay of Marmaris and also has a great lighting system in place so even the shite spots that had appeared right on cue, would not be noticed. Good choice don't you think? The NLP dude certainly thought so as instead of making conversation, he was looking far, far into the distance in a way that I can only describe as sheer boredom. I later found out that as I thought, the bloke is painfully shy and also doesn't speak English as well as I had remembered, so it made for a bit of a difficult evening. However, the vodka was flowing, for me anyway as he was on redbull alone. I nearly choked when he ordered a plain redbull, I mean how totally odd not to have vodka in it!? So with me half cut and him totally sober, you can only imagine the things I was coming out with. I seem to remember making a really off the cuff remark; 'I really dislike stupid people'. Why I made that remark I will never know as I stopped trying to remember the conversation at about 1am just after I arrived home.

Not a bad night even though I was the one doing all the talking, but that's the story of my life so I am used to it. Am I going to see him again? I don't really want to as we didn't click but I am not able to make a decision on just a few hours on whether or not I like him yet, so I may have to. The ball is now in his court as I refuse to invite myself out for drinks for a second time. I mean that would be downright stupid.

8th June

Dear wannabe socialite that is scared of grasshoppers,

Why me, seriously, why me?

After a rather uneventful day I was glad to take a walk along Marmaris beach front with Lorraine, stopping off for a bite and then tootling on home for a rather uneventful evening that was supposed to go something like this:
-Wash Hair
-Do a bit of work
-Shop on eBay
-Diary Entry
-DVD in bed
-Sleep
I have managed to wash my hair, do a bit of work, shop on eBay, I am completing the diary entry right now, but sleep? Not much chance of that now that I have a lodger. Gucci discovered a grasshopper the size of a plate in my lounge that possibly would have remained undiscovered if he had not tormented the thing into having an eppy fit and making it go crazy hopping all over, and ending up taking pride of place all cosy and snug on the rug. I was just trying to slide off the sofa to go running for cover when Gucci decided that he was not at all happy with this situation. And then the worst happened; Gucci made his main attack. If I thought the eppy fit of seconds before was bad, Christ alive it got even worse as the horrifically huge grasshopper bounced around my lounge finally landing on my big toe. I kid you fucking not. Well, you can just imagine what happened next: The arms and legs went flapping and flailing, the coffee was thrown in the air, the ashtray strewn all over the floor and Gucci hopping up and down with spit, snot and snarl trying to get to the God damn grasshopper, all the while thinking it was the best game ever.

When I eventually got the over enthusiastic Guch off me and grabbed him, the panic set in as there was no grasshopper in sight. I doubt that there will be a good conclusion to this tale as I am now in my bedroom, Guch beside me, not daring to open the bedroom door in the fear that the beast will be there waiting for round two.

If I had a boyfriend, this would all be in hand by now, but sadly this poor terrified Brit has no chance of leaving this bedroom in the hopes of finding one for quite some time. Summer you have a lot to answer for, please piss off and let the winter return...

On the upside, NLP dude has been in touch today asking if I would like to go out again. Now I say that he has been in touch, well actually if truth be told, I text him first. But I didn't invite myself out; this gal has got some pride (occasionally). Instead I told him that I was waiting for him to ask me out. It worked well as he took the hint and indeed asked me out. However after replying asking when, I have not heard back from him since.

Fucker.

10th June

Dear Diary,

OK so I was just sitting here watching a bit of VH1 and trying to ignore the fact that:
a) I'm a saddo for just lying on my sofa watching movie soundtracks, and

b) I may still have the grasshopper lurking around probably watching me watching VH1 also thinking that I am a saddo for watching movie soundtracks,

when my neighbour who lives opposite called me up and asked me what I would be up to when he returned home from work at approx 01.00am. I explained to him that if I was not asleep I would probably be lying on my sofa, bag of crisps in one hand and tissues in the other watching VH1's movie sound tracks. He took that as a cue to ask if he could come round for a drink when he finished work as he was super stressed. Never mind the time being 01.00am and most normal people would be in bed asleep - no, never mind that at all, it's all about *him and his stress*. Why should my being tired effect him wanting to have a drink and de-stress?
You see here in Turkey the concept of time just does not matter to certain people, my neighbour being the prime culprit. For example, after my horrific experience with the grasshopper, Guch and I went to bed early as Guch was shattered from trying to get the bug and I was too scared to stay downstairs any longer. We both drifted off into a panic induced sleep, well I did anyway; Guch was just happy he got to sleep with his Mum therefore abusing the situation and farted right through the night. In fact I smell Guch fart on my bloody clothes right now.
Anyway: back to the point. We were in a deep sleep when my mobile started ringing ridiculously on and on and on and on. There were 11 missed calls from my stupid neighbour; one after the other. If that wasn't enough to send me hurtling out of the bedroom, across the snake infested path and down the insect ridden stairs to his door to knock him out, then him throwing stones at my balcony window certainly would have done the trick. However, my fear overcame my annoyance so I ended up staying put watching my ringing phone continue to ring. Why didn't I answer it and

tell him to piss off? Well that would have encouraged him to come a
knockin' at the door with victory in his eyes knowing that he
had succeeded in waking me up.
Anyhow, he eventually took the hint and buggered off leaving me alone.
Alone and very much awake, the selfish shit.
That is the point that I was trying to make - no consideration for the person
that they are annoying/waking up. It's all about them.

My rude neighbour reminds me a bit of Mr. Attitude in Istanbul. Mr.
Attitude was very much the same - as long as everything was going his way
he didn't care about anything else, in fact even when things were not going
his way, it was still always all about him. You know the type - Know it all's.
Can't friggin' stand them, but I constantly attract them.

So what I am trying to say here in a terribly round about sort of way is why
do people have no consideration anymore? If someone didn't answer the
phone to me after 2 missed calls I can safely say I would give the hell up.
Well, give the hell up calling and turn to texting instead, but at least that is
less invasive.
The time is now 01.15am. If my neighbour calls as he said he would any
time from now onwards, I think I will just invite him over. Why? I don't
want to have another 22,000,000,0000 missed calls waking me the hell up if
I choose to take my sorry arse up to bed soon.
And if he doesn't call, I am going to leave it an hour from now when I
know he will be tucked up in bed and plague the living crap out of him.
The sad fact is that he will probably answer on the first ring and tell me to
piss of cos he is sleeping. Quite right too.

NLP dude update: No news is good news, right?

12th June

Dear self that never learns,

What a weekend. It must have been a good one as I certainly have the thumping head to prove it.

On a good note: NLP dude has text and it seems that we will be going out again. When is another matter, but I am sure it will happen eventually.

Friday turned out to be a bloody good night starting off with dinner with Kaan. I know I have not mentioned him recently as to be honest there has been no update on that situation, however there is now and what a hell of an update it is. I was two hours late for dinner as my hair was just not working with me. I had a bit of a nightmare with it if I'm totally honest, and of course I didn't want to show up for dinner looking like a skip rat. I know he has seen me in worse states however it's just not the point. When I eventually arrived I was up a height and needed vodka immediately to sort my getting ready stress out. So me being me, I ordered two to save time. After his initial annoyance at my thorough lack of time keeping, we had a great chat and a good laugh – no kissing or mention of kissing to be seen or heard. We then hit bar street and went to a gig of a famous Turkish singer. I had no idea of who she was but she was rather good (or was that a side effects of the vodka?). Either way, we had fun. Fun to the point of being flirty and fun to the point of kissing in the middle of the bar with everyone watching, pointing and shaking their heads with disapproving eyes. But it didn't stop there. It should have but it didn't. We carried on this kissing thing all the way down the street and when we were not kissing we were holding hands while we caught our breath.

Why did we do this again? I don't know but I really liked it. I liked it far too much if truth be told. It was hot, passionate, lustful and sexy all rolled into an amazingly seductive snogathon. I would now like to introduce you to my old friend obsession.

I decided to approach the kissing subject with Kaan head on and in broad daylight where there is no fear of more kissing. He was coming to pick me up to take me back to my car that I had abandoned at the restaurant the night before. It was the perfect time to discuss this tricky situation as I was still a little drunk. So we discussed it and that was that. Nothing to get obsessed about right? Wrong. We ended up staying for coffee in the restaurant where we continued to discuss, laugh, flirt but not kiss. It would have been inappropriate to have kissed right there and then even though that's all I could think of doing. This time though we didn't say that we wouldn't do it again. Yes it should be an unspoken rule that we will never go down that road, but I've a sneaky feeling that we will.

Anyway, as I was meeting friends for drinks I had to leave. What I actually wanted to do was just sit there and snog all day and all night, but plans were plans.

Drinks were definitely called for as by the time I had analysed and obsessed the living crap out of the situation, my head was up my arse. So drink I did. Drink and talk it out with my friends. Funnily enough they all said the same: do not go there again under any circumstances. They are right, I know I should not continue with this kissing saga, but it has gone past the point of just kissing because now the obsession is setting in. Shit. Then in the midst of deep conversation with my friends, I received a text message. It was from him. No words, just a smiley face. He was thinking about me too...

I knew where he was going to be, so I made up a story of why we needed to go to this particular bar, and off we all went. And there he was. It was like magnets and electricity with a dash of vodka for good measure. As I walked over I imagined him just grabbing me, kissing me and declaring his undying love to me. Of course what actually happened was I walked over and as we didn't quite know what to say to each other, we laughed. It would just have to do. Obviously I couldn't stand with him all night making goo goo eyes as my friends would have shot me, so I went back to my friends and yet more vodka.

The night was a good one and one by one my friends went home which left me wanting to stay and kiss. I stayed but I didn't kiss. We had a drink together and I think it's safe to say that we both like each other. But that is a point that will never be discussed. Not ever. It just can't be. But if it could be, what would I want to do? I tell you what I would want to do, I would want to stop talking and start kissing. And that's why it is never to be discussed as nothing good can ever come of this and I need to stop thinking about kissing him.

I need a diversion and fast as I have just arranged another vodka night with him for this week. There may be trouble ahead as I am going into this with my eyes wide open and hope flooding my mind.

Like I have already said: nothing good can ever come of this.

In other news the NLP dude has gone to Izmir this week and when he gets back I am going to man up and kiss him to see if there is anything at all there. I very much doubt it now but needs must. And I promise I won't be thinking about Kaan whilst doing it.

14th June

Dear diversion seeker,

OK, so firstly I have come to the decision that the chemistry with NLP dude isn't really there, as much as I was kidding myself that it could be, it just isn't. And without chemistry, you got nothing. Chemistry is not the issue with my kissing friend Kaan though. There is certainly bucket's full of chemistry there and that scares the living crap out of me as he is already spoken for. This doesn't help me in the diversion that I so desperately require though does it?

I have done rather well though; I have not over obsessed about Kaan. I have not imagined us running off into the sunset to be happy for the rest of our days. I have not imagined the big white wedding or the holidays we could take. I have not imagined that the universe has brought together two long lost mates and I have certainly not imagined having his children. Oh dear god. Houston, we have a problem.

I have however been asked out on a date by another young, virile, very good looking, snappy dressing suitor. He doesn't speak any English, however I am sure I can get around that as he is just so damn fit. I actually told you about him when I first saw him a few weeks ago whilst I was in the hairdressers getting my roots sorted out. I asked his friend about him, and then indulged in a lot of Facebook perving. I didn't request him as a friend as sometimes I can refrain you know. Anyway, after I had finished obsessing about him, I promptly forgot about him. Now all of a sudden he gets in touch and asks me out. Is it me or is that a bit odd? I guess I will never know unless I go out with him tomorrow night as arranged. I am just hoping and praying that I don't talk myself out of it as this is the kind of diversion that I need, and as he is a sexy diversion, what am I moaning about? Jeeze it's only a date after all! Sometimes I need to give myself somewhat of a slap as I over dramatize damn near everything. I do this because here in Marmaris I have seen a lot of things go on that make you put the brick wall well and truly up and in turn this gives you ridiculously huge trust issues. Is the brick wall worth it at the age of 30 and *still* single? Damn right it's worth it. Self preservation is the key to living here. Does Marmaris make you hard faced? Yes, it most certainly does. Marmaris and ex boyfriends anyway. But I have not lost hope. If one day I was to lose everything but was still left with hope, then that's good enough for me.

So; no more of this talking myself out of going on the date crap. I am going and yes there is going to be amazing chemistry (cos of his hotness), and if there isn't, well there is always vodka...

P.S I had a dream that I married my ex last night. Then when I went onto Facebook to change my status to 'Married to', he didn't accept the request and his status remained as single.

What is that one trying to tell me then?

16th June

Dear dater gal,

I went on the date last night. Yes I forced myself out of the door, down to Jess's hotel to drink some Dutch courage and wait for my date to arrive. I decided to take Jess and her boyfriend along with me on my date as the English (or lack of it on his part) was going to be a bit of an issue and everyone in the world speaks better Turkish than I do. The English was an issue but that didn't stop me perving all over him in sheer lust. Yes the boy is a looker, a sharp dresser, in my age group and has severe determination to learn English. Sod the English, body talk would work just fine, however the boy is a gentleman (God damn him).
We had an excellent three way conversation and it was not awkward at all, in fact I was laughing for most of the night! Hallelujah!
He is not a player (so he says), he wants to get married, he is saving to open up his own business and did I mention that he is friggin' gorgeous?
Even Jess the Minger has got good vibes about him and that says an awful lot as she has vetted some of the things that I have introduced to her in the past and she is generally right on the money.
He definitely has his green light turned on and has come to that time in his life (as all men eventually do) where he feels it is time to settle down.
What great luck I seem to have finally stumbled upon! In fact I shall pat myself on the back.
What's that now, don't speak too soon? Piss off, I'm going to revel in this as he is damn near perfect all apart from the language barrier. However, he says give him two months and he will most definitely be rattling off conversations about quantum physics with me :) And I believe him too.

Oh I do so love this stage, when I have just started to date someone and the tummy is filled with butterflies, the excitement in the pit of the stomach, the nerves, well everything really ☺ I think I like this one!
Also due to the copious amounts of Dutch courage consumed, my brick wall was not as high as it normally is, and I didn't scare him off!
Yey!
I suppose you could label me 'Smitten' right now.

Oh yeah, and he likes horrifically naughty dogs too. Thank God as Gucci was nearly getting sold! (Said whilst looking at a horrifically naughty dog, smiling whilst he does his best frog impression.)

20th June

Dear Karma,

As I sit here half watching 'My name is Earl' and half contemplating about inviting my new suitor over, I started to think about Karma and how it should work in good ways if you are generally speaking a good person. What am I talking about? My weekend of debauchery that's what.

All the ingredients were there to make it one of greatness:
-Alcohol
-Mingers
-Hed Kandi
-BBQ's
-More Alcohol
- Randomness
Not much more a single wannabe socialite could ask for really.
Friday turned out to be an unexpected night to say the least. I was expecting to be having vodka night with Kaan, but he cancelled at last minute. So I was left at a bit of a loose end. Not for long though due to being cajoled by Jess into partying my arse off to the tunes of Hed Kandi. I can never say no and even though I had no idea what the hell Hed Kandi was before I arrived at the club, I certainly did by the end of it.
Wicked.com
And my snappy dressing suitor was right there with us.

We drank, danced, took random photos, piled back to mine and drank some more.
Then it all went a bit Pete Tong. The full would take the next two hours to tell you, so let me give you the shortened version;
Jess and I ended up in the cemetery at 8am, mugs of vodka in hand, pyjamas on, commenting on just how peaceful it was there at that time of day. Why? Jess's Mum is buried there and due to us having another 'it's time to face life' chat we decided to do just that in the garden of the dead. Scary Fact. All the while the new suitor was waiting patiently at home for me to come back.
Sucker? We have to put them through trials don't we, otherwise how do we

know how much it will take to crack these new suitors?

When I eventually made it home I found new suitor asleep on the sofa with Gucci. I would have left him there had he not have woken up with a naughty glint in his eye. Need I say anymore?
Trial 1 Status: Completed Successfully ;)

Saturday kicked off with Eastenders (I missed the first episode as I decided to ignore the alarm due to my shagathon undertaken at 9.30am, then went back to sleep for a while in preparation for dinner and drinks with the Mingers. Good times.

Sunday was another good day. The new suitor came over for a pool day and I even got my belly out in front of him! Then team Minger showed the new suitor exactly how it's done with a Sunday with Beer and BBQ night. Yes all *seemed* well on the western front.
Alas, as I usually do, I spoke to soon. Today I started getting bombarded with texts from the new suitor. Why is it that they just don't know when to stop over here?
I like the air of mystery and sometimes I like to do a bit of the chasing just to kick start my obsession. But will they let us do that? No...
I'm really hoping that this doesn't put me off my new suitor as once I have gone off someone there ain't no getting those first initial butterflies back again. Unfortunately: Fact.

If karma were here with me now it would do its damndest to make sure that nothing puts me off the cute snappy dressing new suitor.
Karma would have shown up when he spouted 'you will not drink as much anymore' and stopped those words dead in their tracks before escaping from said suitor's mouth.
Karma would teach him English in a day (or at least teach me Turkish).
Karma would have me wanting to spend every waking moment with my new suitor in the first flushes of romance and would take Kaan my kissing friend out of my troubled mind.
Karma coulda, woulda, shoulda. But didn't.

So as the weekend fades into a distant memory, my impending doom has

not hit me as fast as it usually would on this boring Monday night.
I am certainly not saying that it won't arrive at some point, but so far so
good.

And to top it all off, Betty my dear scooter was stolen on Friday night right
from my drive way. What the bloody bollocks have I done to deserve that
one then?

Karma. If it was a human, I would slap it. Fact.

24ᵗʰ June

Dear Karma once again,

Seriously, will I never learn (apparently not). After Monday's diary entry on Karma, a normal person would have started to pay attention to Karma and the way it works. Obviously I'm some sort of nob and I didn't, and things started to go to from bad to worse.

I told the new suitor that I needed a good rest on Monday night meaning that we would not be seeing each other. It is never good when they move in after the first date like they do over here, and after my Ex, I vowed I would never let that happen again.
I was quite happy with my 'easy does it' approach, plus I was shattered and wanted to jump straight into bed after 'Made in Chelsea' for a good long kip. Whether it was the language barrier or whether he just couldn't face to be alone without me for one single night again, I did not get the kip that I sorely craved. Nope. What I got was woken up with banging at the front door at 02.30am. At first I ignored it. That was until my phone started going bezerk and Gucci started having a spaz attack as he thought someone was here to take him out for a walk. I would have continued ignoring it but then the shouting started 'Leeeeeeeeiiiiiiiiiiiiiiiiiiiiiiiiiiii!',
'Leeeeeeeeeeeeeeeeeiiiiiiiiiiiiiiiiiiiiiiiiiiiiiiiiiiiiiii!'
As I live in a well respected area with my landlords living right next door, I nearly broke my neck running down the stairs trying to get to the front door before he started yowling again. What happened next was a shock to me as I was expecting to just shut him up and send him away with a flea in his ear, but as I answered the door I felt blind rage creeping across the whole of my entire being resulting in me screaming blue murder waking up everyone in my block.
He huffed and puffed a bit and then buggered off due to the lack of understanding of my English ranting, leaving me with the glaring eyes of all my neighbours. Fucking marvellous. This was a first as usually it is the neighbours and I conspiring how to get rid of all the noise makers in our block, not the other way around. I was totally out of my comfort zone and felt rather embarrassed finding myself at this end of this stick.

Damn the new suitor for waking up the beast within!

After apologizing profusely to the neighbours I took my disgraced self up to bed with the hopes of drifting back off to sleep. Funny how hopes can be shattered isn't it.

When I awoke, I felt really awful, not just about the neighbour situation, but also for unleashing the beast upon my new suitor as I had found out that all he wanted was his wallet that he had forgotten in my house the day before. But still, did it mean that he had to come at 02.30am for it? Apparently yes as time has no boundaries as we already know.

We have made it up now (Just) as I seem to have gotten through to him that if he had come two hours earlier it would not have been as much of an issue. He said he understood, but time will tell on that one won't it.

We actually had fun last night with Jess and her fella, and even managed to cast the image of the previous night into less than a thought. That was until the new suitor and I came back to my house, fell into a deep sleep, then were rudely awoken when the door bell started going at 04.00am. I looked over and he was still in bed, so who the hell was that then? Oh dear, I could feel the beast within starting to stir again and I knew that this was not going to be pretty.

I answered the door to find two of last night's neighbours glaring at me telling me that my car had parked theirs in. So with all the might that I could muster, I stomped down to the car, muttering obscenities the whole way and shifted Kastro out of their way.

And with that, I stomped back up to my bed with the flea in my ear that was supposed to belong to my new suitor two nights previously.

KARMA! Dont you just love it?

27th June

Dear Queen,

I am sitting here writing this whilst I have the theme tune to my life playing: Yes Queen it's one of yours, a mighty fine one actually - 'another one bites the dust'.

Yes the weekend has proven to be one where true colours are brought out in the brightest of forms. I shouldn't be surprised, but sadly I am.

On Friday night, the new suitor came to my house. I must say, we had a great night, we laughed and laughed and in general, it was one of those good nights that make you kinda swoon. Until he asked for a fucking key. And yes, just to clarify, I mean a key to my apartment. We had been dating for all of 8 days.

It's OK, let the shock waves flow. I did.

I didn't say anything. I didn't say no and I didn't say yes. I was in shock after all, so all I did was umm and ahh about possibly having a spare key somewhere but I didn't know where.

Saturday brought even more new colours. Jess wanted to go to bar street as she had split up with the boyfriend (again) and was on a frigging mission. I asked the new suitor if he wanted to come and he said he didn't fancy bar street but would come and meet me at the hotel before that for a few drinks. Fair enough I thought.

Then he text asking if I missed him.

I am not a gal that dishes out the feelings left right and centre and I also don't make shit up. I am more of a 'let's wait at least a month' kind of sort, so I replied to the text with *Maybe (and that was a reach)*. I was only playing, but he obviously didn't quite get it and said that *maybe* instead of coming to the hotel to meet up, he would just go home instead.

Fair enough once again I thought, and told him so. As you can see, I was not taking the bait and I was certainly not about to fall into the pit that he so desperately wanted to trap me in. We did not meet that night, nor did I drunk text stalk him when I got home at 5am. Bravo me!

Note: I clearly am not as enamoured with this one as I originally thought.

I did text him on the Sunday and we arranged that after he finished work he would come over and we would eat together. No problem there, in fact I was looking forward to it, until he asked if I had located the dreaded key… Yep the time had come for me to lay the cards on the table and tell him that he was not going to get the key. In actual fact what I text him was that if we were still together in nine months or so, maybe he would get the key then, all being well of course. Pretty normal I thought? He obviously didn't as what I got as a reply was rather rude and pissed me right off: "If you think like this you are selfish and I don't want you". What excellent train of thought… Dick head.

Not biting again, all he got in response to that was "OK Goodbye".

I decided to call on Jess for a bit of advice. You see I do like him but I was not giving up the key for love nor money after eight days of dating. This to me is pure craziness.

We decided that I would send one last message saying that if he wanted to finish the '*relationship*' over this then it is just ridiculous. He text back telling me that he would be at my house at 12.30am. No he bloody wouldn't! Why does he not get it? Am I being unreasonable here? I replied letting him know that we would just talk tomorrow instead, to which I got no reply. Jess convinced me not to text again that night and I actually managed to take her advice. I text today instead asking how he was. I got a reply so it was all good, or so I thought… Later on he asked what I was doing tonight, so I told him I was home and if he wanted to come over to *talk*, he could. At that point Pete Tong arrived. Yes, as I should have known, it all went a bit wrong in so many terrible ways.

He told me that he was hungry and that *I* was to buy him a Pizza (and a mixed one at that). The beast of rage started to stir within once again and even before I sent the next text to him I knew that I could not control my sheer fury.

So in the nicest possible way I told him I was not here to buy him Pizza's and/or look after him in any way shape or form, but if he wanted to talk, then he could still come round.

What reply did I get you may wonder? "I am tired, I want to sleep early, see you tomorrow".

I should have considered stopping there, but you guessed it, I didn't.

Without skipping a beat my fingers were doing the talking, tapping out the next text. I didn't let him have it; I decided to hold back a bit. I told him that a girl of 30 years old is over game playing and the games that he is playing can get shoved up his arse along with his head.

Like I said, I didn't let him have it, but as I sit here contemplating letting him have it, I just can't be bothered wasting the one minute it would take to type out the text as I believe I have already wasted eight days of being taken for some sort of chump.

So in conclusion, his devious plan did not work, nor will any plan like that ever work with a girl like me that has seen it all before...

Thinking back, I should have never brought him back to my pad with the gang nine days ago. Why? Well, my pad is quite nice, not your normal run of the mill Turkish apartment, a bit more UK stylee and anyone that walks through the door would think the same as he probably did: 'I'm onto a winner here'. Whether I have money or whether I chose to decorate my pad with the last of my money, no snappy dressing suitor will ever be onto a winner or have an easy ride with this gal in the driving seat.

I am nobody's fool and what I have, I have worked damn hard for and won't give it up for a jumped up little stud wannabe.

Have I learnt a lesson here? Yes, I believe another life lesson has been thoroughly learnt. Thank you universe for the past few days teaching me that there are still some jumped up tits out there that can pull the wool over my eyes with their snappy dressing and smooth moves that I thought I was most definitely immune to. Thank you universe for letting me have a bloody lucky escape. And thank you universe for showing me that I am not desperate enough to fall for the shit this one was trying to flush.

And finally, I am thinking that it might be time to move on from Turkey. Not because of the guy in case you wondered. This thought started to creep over me last year and I seem to keep getting subtle nudges from the universe that yes it is indeed time to really think about the next step. What is the next step for this single wannabe socialite?

Well I am unsure as yet but I know it does not involve going back to the UK. Other than that, I am open to suggestions.

I just hope and pray that this is not all there is. I hope and pray that there is more left for me than what I have been dished up so far, as if this really is all there is, then please just stick a fork in me cos in the nicest possible way - I'm done.

Chapter 4 – July 2011

2nd July

Dear vegetable formerly known as Lei,

This week has been rather mental to say the least. After Monday's entry I managed to cheer myself up by taking part in some very random things.

Mental Note for the Future: Take part in more random crap as it really can cheer up the most miserable of Mingers.

Random Occurrence 1: On Tuesday I found myself in a situation that I was unable to say no to; I was roped into hosting Bingo and a quiz in one of the hotels I work with. I have not hosted bingo since I worked a winter season as a Rep in Portugal back in 2002, so I can't say I was looking forward to it. Quizzes are easy, but the Bingo crowd bloody well berate you if you don't call all the numbers by their special names. Two fat ladies 88 is just about all I can remember right now and that's only because I resemble one. Bingo goers really are the crème de la crème of mo fo's when you are trying to host an evening as they are just so damn serious about it. They even bring their own Bingo dabbers on holiday! I got through the night with quite a few mishaps but generally the crowd was good to me. Not sure what they said behind my back, but to my face they were OK.

On Wednesday Kaan suggested an impromptu vodka night at my house that I jumped at. Due to already being dumped once this week I really needed a pick me up and Kaan always manages to give me that.

The vodka was working well and Kaan was on good form, just what the doctor ordered. We were full swing of vodka night when the snappy dressing ex suitor showed up at my door unannounced. Somehow I knew that I hadn't seen the last of that tit. Uncomfortable.com.

Firstly Kaan must have felt rather uncomfortable, and secondly I had not drunk near enough vodka to deal with the ex suitor, the drama and his lack of English... I really wanted him to just piss off as he was interrupting my good time but I was also intrigued as to why he was here. I felt a bit weird about it but ended up inviting him in. As you have probably guessed, he was not particularly struck on the idea of seeing my male vodka drinking companion sitting rather comfortably on the sofa. Getoverit.com. Awkwardness filled the room with its vibes, and with that I knew another vodka was required to get me through this ridiculous situation. And that's how it went down; in a mist of booze he informed me (with the help of Kaan translating) that he wants to get back together.

Whaaaaaaaaaaaaattttttttttttttttt? Whyyyyyyyyyyyyy!!!????? I think 8 days worth of him was quite long enough! Why the hell would *he* even want more? And after all the shite names he called me too! There was nothing left for it but to try and have my say about the whole key/pizza situation. Thankfully Kaan helped out on that score too. I managed to get my point across but I don't think everything that I said was translated as I could see the look on Kaan's face at some of the things that I was coming out with. Thinking things through properly now, I just knew that if the roles were reversed I would have wisely chosen only certain points to translate too.

And with that, vodka night continued. With Kaan and with the snappy dressing ex suitor. Only when the vodka had run out and there was not a drop of alcohol left in the house did Kaan leave. The suitor? That fucker stayed ;) One may say that I bring everything on myself, but the boy is just so fit.

Thursday brought another hangover and Random Occurrence 2: Stupid hung-over girl with far too much work to get through before having to host a karaoke evening (Yes you heard me right, and with my voice, whatever next!). Well only one thing for it right, beer. Reading this in future times I will possibly assume that I am some sort of raging alki, so let me make this clear here and now – Future self, I am a social drinker only. It just so happens that when single in the summer, being social is a near nightly occurrence.

Back to the Karaoke: I didn't know that getting people up to sing would be such a hard task that would require me having to sing first. Had I of known this I possibly would have chickened out of going. I possibly wouldn't have had the great night that I had and I possibly would have woken up on Friday morning without the hangover. It's the "Sliding Doors" theory isn't it. But, I didn't know that I was required to sing first, and I didn't know that I would need to be half cut to get up and do it due to huge amounts of nerves getting the better of me. I didn't know that my voice was as shocking as it was and I didn't know that I would enjoy it so much! And after the karaoke? Yes, the suitor came around again. He turned out to be an excellent aid in my repetitive grasshopper issues.

Friday was a bitch; I was totally right on the hangover front. Why do I insist upon doing this to myself? I'll tell you why, cos I live in a holiday resort and sometimes if you can't beat em, you may as well join em.

Random Occurrence 3: I knew I had to pull it together as I was being taken out for dinner and drinks by one of the five people that have stumbled upon my blog. Weird right? The blog reader happens to be a 27 year old Yanki male named Tim and being that he is American and not Afghan, I found this rather comforting in the safety stakes. I was considering calling it off as it's just a bit weird, but I have done weirder things, so thought I sod it and went along anyway.
This could have turned out to be a disastrous evening. Tim the Yanki could have been an ole pervy dude, or the night could have been super awkward with huge amounts of silence, lots of looking around, fiddling with the tooth picks, etc. Even worse, I could have been raped and murdered. As you can see, neither of those happened as I am alive and well and writing about it.
What I found instead of the pervy dude was rather a lot of interesting conversation, Brandy, Mojito's, more Brandy and very good company.

Tim the Yanki; Interesting.

Tim is not so much of a fitty but he had great conversation and that counts for a lot. I think Tim and I may have clicked a little bit. It certainly didn't hurt that he is a captain of a yacht and a bit rich. Although I didn't really fancy him, I liked him… Put it this way, he is not slim, yet he is also not fat; let's settle for chunky. He is tall and chunky / masculine and treats a lady like a lady. He even managed to treat me like a lady and that can be a rather hard task at times. He reminded me of the sort that say 'maam' in that lovely southern drawl. OK so his drawl was not really Alabama southern, but it was sexy (ish). I think it is safe to say that I quite liked Tim. But is it going to matter that I don't really fancy him? Well, we shall see wont we.

Time disappeared into a cloud of what I can only say turned into a yet another fucking hangover. Tim looked after me well. He footed the bill for the expensive dinner on the marina where you generally only find the Marmaris elite dining out, and then the rooftop cocktails in the old town of Marmaris overlooking the cute old fashioned streets with their whitewashed houses, and finally the outrageously expensive drinks down bar street. We didn't kiss though. I didn't fancy him enough for that, but I am not crossing it off my 'to do list' just yet.

Alas, Tim is leaving when the refurbishment of the yacht is complete so even when snappy dressing ex suitor and I fall out again, I probably wouldn't take up with ole Timbo anyway. A woman in every port and all that, plus he wasn't really my type.

So what potentially could have been an awkward as arse evening was a rather good night instead.
#Pleasantlysurprised

4th July

Dear Independence Day,

Ok so even though we Brits do not celebrate Independence Day as a national holiday, it didn't stop me giving myself a half day off work to meet up with Connor an old rep friend of mine that was over from Bodrum for a few hours. Why is it that when Ex Reps get together there is always beer involved? As you can see, I have not collapsed into a drunken pit with sick all over myself as I happen to be here writing about it. Pat on the back to me! More like pat on the back to Connor's friend for making him get back on the bus and go back to Bodrum at a decent hour!

Independence Day has also brought with it another invitation from Tim the Yanki to have what seems like some sort of date on Wednesday night. Correct me if I am wrong, but this certainly sound like a date to me: "How does Pizza, Beer, a laid back American and a fun night sound to you?" I have been known to read things terribly wrong, but I am pretty sure that this one sounds like a bit of a date, right? Conundrum alert! Yes I kind of like Tim, but he is leaving in the not too distant future so what he is probably looking for is a bit of slap and tickle right? Firstly I don't give up slap and tickle too easily these days without knowing that it is going somewhere, and secondly I still don't fancy him. What is a girl to do when it acts like a duck and quacks like a duck? I don't know why I am wowling on about this as I happen to have already accepted Tim's invitation of the beer and pizza night on Wednesday.

By the way, I have not told a that the ex suitor is back on the scene and that's the way it is going to stay. I'm sure he will be leaving the scene pretty soon again anyway. If the truth be told, I am not really feeling the connection with him at all now, not after the inordinate amount of shite he comes out with. I really fancied him at first but now his annoying traits are getting worse. The fucker has started to mimic me. This may be due to the fact that we seriously can't understand each other, or he could just be an irritating sod; either way, I don't like being mimicked. I have asked him to stop and he won't. So. He has also started grabbing my face really hard and pinching my cheeks like I am some sort of young school kid. This is quite normal for Turkish guys to do when showing affection, but by Christ it hurts and I find it offensive. I suppose I am quite stuck in my ways being that I have been single for almost 3 years. I just like things the way I like them and when he drops fag ash on my floor accidently then makes no effort to clean it up, this makes see red. Didn't his Mother teach him how not to be a twat? He also mentioned last night that he now does not believe that he will have mastered conversational English in two months. Bonus as this gives me reason to end this somewhat silly affair. Apparently I had told him that if he had not mastered English in that time frame that I was upping sticks to America, and this was way before Tim the Yanki was on the scene.

And with that, I am going to smoke a fag, dig up my fortune teller's notes and ponder about life whilst trying to catch up on some rest as I have a friend arriving from my old repping days and I can see that this ex rep now RAF man will certainly put me through my paces partying wise...

Shit the bed, the drinking will start again.

14th July

Dear dumped.com,

OK first things first, I have finally been dumped by the ex suitor. Again. Well, I say dumped but it was done in such a nice way. He had a friend of his Facebook me in English saying that he thought I was great but the language barrier was just too much and he couldn't do it. He wished me all the best, as I did to him, and that's that. Fancy getting someone else to dump me over facebook eh? I really didn't mind, and for fucks sake it was about time.

If it had stayed at 'that's that' it would have been great, but it didn't wouldn't you know it. Two days later, whilst I had the Tim the Yanki round for our first DVD date, he started texting me asking if he could come round for a chat. If we could actually chat life would be great, however google translate doesn't translate paragraphs too well. So I told him no to the chat and consequently got bombarded with awful Turkish messages which even google translate refused to have a go at. Must have been bad ones then eh? Finally I got one in English saying: 'You always do this, you are selfish, we are finished and I hate you'. Seriously, what the fucking fuck? Hadn't I already been dumped a few days earlier in the week? No? Must have been me then…

On to Timbo the Yanki: I find it a necessity to include here that although we had a nice night, I still do not fancy him. He is good conversation and I am hoping that this will overcome the non fancying status. Actually, beer overcame this status as he stayed over. Yes in my bed. The earth did not move and his kissing is simply shit, but I'm hoping we can work on that. I just wish that I could fancy him.

And finally onto my friend Nigel's arrival: Since he arrived I seem to have found myself going back in time to when we drank until morning, had an hours sleep, went to work, went home for a shower to do it all over again. This time round though we don't seem to be fairing as well as we are both seven years older and require extra recovery time.

If I ever wondered if I could be a rep again, I now know the answer is irreverently no. In fact, I wouldn't want to be even if I was a few years younger. Going into repping is not like going into a normal job, it is going into a lifestyle. If your lifestyle does not involve getting spoken to like a piece of shit by customers on a daily basis, socializing with people that you would never ever dream of socialising with at home, you don't like booze and you don't want to work every hour that god gives; then this lifestyle is not for you. If I had to do my time again, could I do it? Not at the merry old age of 30 that's for sure.

But enough of that, what I really need to tell you about is what I have actually been up to since Monday's arrival of Nigel... When he finally arrived at 5am he didn't give himself much recuperation time as the next morning he was up with the larks (the tit), whilst I struggled to make it through the day. I seriously have started to realize that a girl of 30 years and older needs at least 10 hours of sleep a night to function and feel less zombie like and more socialite.

Alas, there was no escaping Nigel's first night of holiday drinking, and off course we hit the town, zimmer frames and all.

Tim the Yanki and his stupid Yanki friend joined the fellowship of alcohol gang, and even though I didn't think that I was particularly drunk, I bloody well must have been as I seem to recall arguing with Yanki's pal re vegetarianism and also inviting anyone that would listen to join in my karaoke night on Thursday.

Can I just point out that Tim the Yanki has also started to show some irritating qualities. This started on our first DVD date night, and also on the night that Nigel arrived whilst he was keeping me company. I just can't put my finger on why he seems to be irritating me so; maybe it's due to the fact that he seems to know everything. Why do I always attract them! My British ex fiancée (yes someone proposed to me once), is another one to add to the list there. And I swear that if the snappy dressing ex suitor could have spoken English, he too would have made that list. I'm giving Tim the benefit of the doubt for now, but is it bad that I find him irritating so early on? Bugger it, he's leaving soon, I can put up and shut up for the time being.

Tuesday started off with a hangover and a half. Then I turned on the work email and Christ alive I could have died. Over 100 emails sitting there waiting to be answered. Not my proudest day on the planet let me tell you. One email caught my eye though. Not so much of a work email but a request email from a website that I am a member of where you can advertise and rent your room out to travellers. To be honest I had forgotten that I was a part of that site as I very rarely check it. The email was from a French guy and his American friend requesting to book my spare room over night. Due to Nigel being here, booking the room was a no go, however I had suggested some alternatives, and with that, the French guy suggested drinks. Seeing as though I had previously decided to accept random requests, I agreed to the drinks as Nigel and I were going out anyway, so may as well tie it all in with one shot and a few drinks in bar street. And that's just what we did.

The French guy was friggin' gorgeous and I happened to like him a lot. Bit of an understatement actually as I friggin' bummed off him. I would have had his babies (and I don't even like them). If he had asked for my hand in marriage, I would have accepted immediately. Stat. Yep I have a crush and I have it bad. If only Nigel was not here they would have booked my house. So in retrospect, I would have been paid to perv. Fucking Nigel. Tim? Tim who? Seriously, pass me the French dude please!

Meeting people that I wouldn't normally meet in less than normal circumstances has opened my eyes to a world that exists outside of Marmaris. Here we live in a bubble and if you don't pop it, it can be very hard to imagine that life goes on outside of this bubble.
I find myself itching to leave the bubble, just for a while, and find more random people in more random places. I really should start putting a plan into action for getting out of the rut that I seem to be stuck in and go travelling. Maybe France should be on my hit list then? After all, I do need a break. A break in the arms of my new Romeo ;)
Oh Lei you are a right nob. I didn't even kiss the boy. I wanted to, and it certainly seemed that he fancied a snog too. How do I know? Being French he was very forth coming and in the dirtiest of sexy French accents he said 'Kiss me Lei, I want you tonight'. Honest to god. And with that, I ran off into the night just like Cinder-frikkin-ella. Why? As mentioned above, because I am a right nob. Thank god for Facebook as the fit French boy added me the very next day. Shame he had already disappeared off to Istanbul…Should I just buy a ticket to Istanbul then? I'm sure Nigel would

love to see a bit of it.

On Wednesday I thankfully convinced Nigel not to go out and party. Not much convincing needed actually as he refused to leave his room for the full day. His tiredness and hangover were holding him hostage.
Being the hostess that I am, I decided to cook a mean veggie lasagne and dragged Nigel out of his room for just long enough to eat and watch a movie. Poor sod was a sick puppy indeed.

Thursday came and I hosted the karaoke evening. Thankfully I only had to sing once. You could say that I saved the ear drums of mankind that evening by only singing once. Funny how when someone is a God awful singer it encourages others to fill out their request slips and hand them in just to prove that they are indeed a better singer than the actual host. Fuckers. Anyway, it was a good night what with Nigel trying to pull every woman in sight, the Yanki showing up, and me with my blistered heels due to wearing the most horrifically uncomfortable shoes known to man (but when they look that good, allowances need to be made). Yep, so far so good. We hit the beach front after the Karaoke for a few more drinks. More events occurred. I guess there are differences between us Brits and Yanki's after all, and fuelled with alcohol I could have possibly come across as a bit rude. Actually, let's be honest here: I was very rude and I know it, but I do have an odd sense of humour and the Yanki was definitely irritating me. Bloody know it all's.
After we could not drink anymore, it was off to the soup kitchen for end of night refreshments. This is where is started to spiral down the path of no return. My friends know that my sense of humour is plain weird (especially when pissed), but people that don't really know me well (i.e. the Yanki) could possibly feel that I was being rather offensive when I decided to take the hugest swig of water and proceeded to spit it right in the Yanki's face. I was creased up in the largest amount of giggles, but alas, the Yanki was not. I just could not understand why the look of sheer fury was looming across his face making the vain on his forehead pop out like I had never seen it pop before (even during the crap sex we had been having). Needless to say, this made me worse on the laughter front.
I was literally in full swing of rip roaring, tear dripping, uncontrollable red faced laughter. The Yanki was still not. In fact he actually got up and left.

The night ended with Nigel and l going home (me crying with laughter all the way) to a hot as hell house and falling asleep with the air con on, waking up thinking that I had magically transported to Iceland.

Friday arrived. Did I feel guilty about spitting water all over the Yanki? No, as I am still fuelled with laughter about the situation.
I had pre-warned the dude that when drunk I do things for personal amusement, so really he knew what he was letting himself in for.
Thankfully Nigel was not up for going out so we had a nice DVD night with loads of food and munchies.

Saturday brought good times once again.
My Mum skyped and told me that I am blogging far too much about my alcohol fuelled nights. My answer to that is how do you escape it when you have a house guest that is here to go out and party? Being South African, my Mum is a bit different to most other Mums I know. She likes to write on my Facebook wall things that should be kept to a private message and sometimes she even tells my friends off for swearing. She doesn't know it, but she has a bit of a following with my friends waiting to see what she will say next, what with commenting on my photos telling me I look hideous, and making comments about how she does not want a dead child, etc, it makes for entertaining reading for my friends. They write things now just to annoy her into action.
And yes, she has commented on my blog a few times too. I wonder what she would say about this very diary? Once again Mum, if you are reading this, put it bloody well down now.

Anyway, back to the story. Being Saturday night we hooked up with Kaan in bar street and I proceeded to test a point. I wanted to check that I was not mental in the head, so once again I found myself taking a great big gulp of liquid (Vodka this time) and spitting it at my dear kissing pal. God I'm such a fucking tit when I'm drunk. I see that now. However, Kaan didn't skip a beat when taking a gulp of his own drink and doing the same back to me. In fits of laughter, we both stood there dripping in drink in the middle of the club thinking it was the funniest thing that ever could have happened.
Point proved - I am not mentally challenged. However I am a wanker.

When we moved onto B52s the music was banging and the atmosphere was jumping, as was the crowd. I bumped into an old but good pal of mine that now lives in the UK. Putting it mildly, I was ecstatic to see him. He is a friend that vodka nights originally started with and true to form we were also snogging buddies. I have arranged to meet up with him soon for a good old fashioned catch up. Can't say I fancy him anymore, but he was never a looker in my eyes anyway, it was his personality that got my attention.

Then Kaan pointed out that my bastard ex was in the vicinity. He looked a right ole state. His hair was all long and curly and minging, he looked shorter than I remember and basically, he looked really shit. Nigel's jaw was literally hanging open; he could not believe that the guy I had been going on about since his arrival looked like a tramp. Each to their own I suppose. Thankfully he didn't come over and I wasn't drunk enough to be nice or dish out abuse, so we settled on heading to the soup kitchen to feed our faces instead. I did not drunk text him from home later and I have not obsessed about him either. His minging new look may have something to do with that. Bravo bastard ex and your new shitty look, Bravo!

Sunday brought a slight hangover but nothing to write home about which made a nice change from the norm. It was just too damn hot to do anything today, so we had a home day that involved movies, pigging out and absolutely no booze at all.

I think I have actually made a bit of a decision. I have decided that I do indeed need to leave Marmaris for a while and travel. Where to is another but Thailand seems to be somewhere that I am toying with. Knowing me the destination may change 100 times before leaving Turkey, but it's all good. A change is as good as a rest so they say...

P.S I had not heard from the Yanki up until tonight when he text: "I am on a terrible double date and need a reason to leave". Fuck off I'm not playing that game you cheeky git! I didn't reply and this must have angered him as I got another text 45 minutes later saying he didn't need me to provide a reason to leave now as someone else had given him one. Nice one tit. As I didn't bite that time either, I got another text: 'Lei, I was very pissed at you for spitting in my face but I have got over it now. If you would like to get a drink then call me as I really like your quirky ways'.

What a wanker. I have gone off him in such a massive way that I now find him ugly. When it's gone, it's gone. I did text him back letting him know that we should just be friends. He responded with a bit of mumbled gumph about hoping that it could go somewhere further than just friends.

I doubt it.

22nd July

Dear thankful liver,

This week has been somewhat slower than last and even though
I haven't really done too much, I needed the break. Seriously I wonder how
I ever was able to party so much without ending up in hospital. I guess
that's age for you, before you know it you're a 70 year old *spinster* with 2 hip
replacements (due to excessive partying), a liver transplant (again down to
the partying) and a penchant for dogs because you thought being single was
the best bet at the time.

I have decided to pose a question and my question is this:
When is it time to box up your stilettos and start wearing flats in the hopes
of landing a decent Man?
I will come back to that later...

On Monday I treated my vampire like skin to a bit of sun. This was a first,
seriously. As I'm more of a night time kinda gal it was an interesting
experience for Nigel and I to head down to the beautiful, quiet and serene
Aktaş area just outside of Marmaris to catch some rays. I adore Marmaris
but it's also so nice to escape the hustle that is, and driving only 10 minutes
out of town over to Aktaş you could easily be on planet paradise. I just
love it there. The beach, the trendy little restaurant bars, the scenery, well
you get the picture, I just love it.
I refused to take my t-shirt off as I deem it really unfair to the general
population to get my tummy out in public. The shock would have killed
people so best to keep the beast nicely covered. Quite right too. Yes, I like
every other woman on this planet have body issues. I personally feel that
my tummy is the largest in the world. Maybe I have some sort of
intolerance like wheat or exercise? A lot of people would say let it just hang
out, however I work so hard on covering it up and making it look
nonexistent that I don't wish to shatter the illusion!
Nigel didn't seem to be suffering from the same affliction whilst flaunting
his rounder figure all over the beach whilst eyeing up the ladies doing his
best 'Joey' impression. He really was determined to pull on this holiday but

so far no luck. Back in the day he had girls falling at his feet. That was the power of the reps uniform; you put it on and can literally pull anyone. Without it the boy was struggling. The silly tit even tried it on with me the other night. He text me from his room to mine asking if I would like some company. Urm no. I may have fancied him once upon a time but now he no longer has the rep uniform he is simply no longer attractive to me. It wasn't the uniform that I liked, it was the confidence that he had whilst wearing it. He doesn't seem to have that anymore, and has replaced it with a beer belly instead. Poor ole Nige.

Nothing really exciting happened during our beach day apart from the ordering of a sodding expensive sandwich and me changing my mind re the Yanki once again. Yes dear diary, I am now regretting telling him that we should be friends. Why did I do it? Well I couldn't be bothered with the drama anymore and when he text about the double date that he had with someone else my nose was pushed out of joint. Yes I know I had mentioned that he was irritating me and that I was kinda bored of him, but I have changed my mind again. It is a woman's prerogative after all. Maybe I'm just clinging onto the fact that he can speak English? Whatever it is I am thinking of getting back on that horse once more. I won't know if it's a bad decision until I do it so I may as well just crack on.

On Tuesday we were going to hit the town however decided a night in would be a wiser idea considering our age and general state of us. I went to bed before midnight and had fallen into a grand old sleep when the ex suitor called at 2am. What did he want? Probably a shag considering the time, however he never got the chance to ask as I was not answering the phone to that issue ridden fool.

Wednesday we went sunbathing again. I say sunbath, but it was more of a play on the slides day whist Nigel tried his shitty luck with the girls once more. Poor bugger struck out again. I however thoroughly enjoyed playing on the slide like the big kid that I am. And yes, the t-shirt was still firmly in place. Kaan joined us for a chat whilst we were sunbathing. I would like to say that I didn't fancy him immediately, but I would be lying. Even though he was in a suit in 100 degree heat, with sweaty pits that had shown through the shirt, I would have snogged him right there and then. I am such a loser.

Thursday came and Nigel went back to the UK. It's let the liver rest time yehaaa! Don't get me wrong, it was a blast having him here, but by god I don't half need a break from life for a while.

Unfortunately I had one more stupid task to get through before I could properly chill out that was due to a rookie mistake I had made with renting my spare room out to a travelling man on business for two nights. I was questioning myself as to whether I had made the right choice, but as it turned out, the man was no problem at all and I got paid on time too, so it worked out quite well. Shame he was not remotely attractive as I could have done with some eye candy to boost this odd mood that I'm in.

Being Thursday I had to go and host the karaoke night. I wasn't sure if I would come back to my belongings with leaving the random stranger in my house, but I had promised to host the sodding night, so host it I would. Plus the Yanki was coming to keep me company.

"What" I hear you ask? Yeah I know, I just can't help myself. Yo-yo much Lei? Make up your damn mind!

This time round I managed to keep my beer in my mouth for a change. #Proudtimes. No snogging though as we are now 'just friends'… Bloody fool. And I mean me by the way.

Its Friday now and I am seriously bored. A boring day all round however a plan has been made to go ice skating with the Yanki tomorrow. One of the hotels has a smallish ice rink and it sounds like fun ;)

I don't have much else to say about today other than I have a random man in my house sitting in the lounge playing with Guch so I have banished myself to the kitchen.

24th July

Dear ice skating self,

The Yanki picked me up at 7pm. As we were going for food first it had to be early. Food was eaten and desert turned into beers while ice skating turned into cocktails. Silly idea thinking that we would make it skating when booze was involved! But if ice skating tastes like mojito's then I really should do it more often.
I found myself being slightly bitchy on more than one occasion. Maybe it was due to coming on my period, or maybe, just maybe it was because he was being his usual irritating self... What is it with me? Why do I keep going out on dates with this dude when I clearly can't stand him? He pays for things yes, but I can pay for my own alcohol. So why do I keep doing it then? Is it because I think that I am going to end up an old spinster and that's why I put myself through such torture?

Anyway, Sunday delivered the edge of darkness.
Today I woke up with a raging hangover and feeling rather sorry for myself as I had no one to keep me entertained. If I had a boyfriend that would be different wouldn't it? The Yanki is not my boyfriend and clearly not likely to be either, but it wouldn't have hurt for him to have taken me out for brunch considering he stayed over last night. How bloody rude...

So this leads me back to the earlier question, the time may have arrived to box up the stilettos but I so don't want to have to start wearing flats in the hopes of landing a half decent man. I can curb my partying yes, but where am I going to meet a half decent bloke if I don't go out and party? It's just a vicious circle isn't it? Some may say that the half decent ones don't hang out in the party atmosphere, but that kind of bloke doesn't hold much appeal to me unfortunately. I like the bad bastards of this world, the tattooed up to the hilt type. Give me a biker dude any day of the week. I also realize that I seriously need to change my breed of bloke if I want a nice one. Or maybe it's me that needs to change? This is harder than I originally thought this landing a decent bloke stuff!

25th July

Dear labyrinth of impending doom,

Please piss off.

Today I have been consumed with the same horrible mood as yesterday. It has me feeling that I am going to be eternally alone. I know it's down to being on my period but for god's sake does it have to be this vile?

I have Facebooked the Yanki to see what he is up to. Guess what he said? He has a friggin' head ache! Stupid Yanki. I even decided to text Kaan for a vodka night. That would be a sure way to cheer me up but it turns out that he is driving to Antalya as we speak. Stupid Kaan. Now I could go out. I actually have somewhere to go but I am not going to due to the principal of it. It's Kimmy's birthday and I had been wondering what she was doing for her birthday for the last week but she had not mentioned it to me so I didn't press it until curiosity got the better of me last night. I Facebooked her to ask if she was doing anything or if it was the case that I was just not invited? She replied and said that off course I am invited and that it's dinner and drinks at 9pm. I chose to ignore her as it really pissed me off that unless I had of contacted her to ask, she would not have invited me. You may be wondering what I have done to be crossed off her birthday list. The answer to that is nothing. Kimmy you see, gets very wrapped up in her work friends and sometimes ignores little old me. I hope she enjoys her fabulous birthday party that I have not been included in and I hope that she chokes on her cake.

As for the bloody Yanki, well he can go and choke on some cake too as I am done playing games now. For fucks sake, I don't even fancy him!

To make matters worse I have just text the NLP dude and he is in bloody Izmir. What is it with everyone leaving Marmaris when I want to do something!

Dam you life! And dam you period!

28th July

Dear happier self,

Looking back over my last diary entry makes me feel like removing it as dear lord above, wasn't I sorry for myself?

I won't delete it as I am a lady (debatable) and I had a period. I possibly should have been locked in a dark room on my own without the laptop though. So with that in mind I am now doom and period free and feel more like the bottle of vodka half full kinda gal that I usually am.

Don't get me wrong, some day's things just don't quite go my way, but I am big enough and ugly enough to take these things on the chin with a shot of Tequila (because it makes me happy and pretty much a heap on the floor). Marmaris gets me down but it also gets me up and I am on the up side of the scale this week (well, so far so good anyway).

So what have I been up to? To let you into a little secret, some terribly awful snogging that's what. My week so far has gone something like this:

On Monday I thought I would wake up feeling on top of the world.

I didn't. I found myself still in the labyrinth of doom, not wanting to leave the house as I may have to talk to someone. I do not wish to discuss Monday anymore.

Finally on Tuesday I woke up feeling nearly me again. It was seriously about time too. I took a drive into town as the Yanki had invited me to take a tour of his boat/yacht/water going vessel that is looking less like the fore mentioned water going vessel and more like a rough draft of Noah's ark. He assured me that indeed they would be leaving on it in full glory to waters filled with less hassle come mid September. Now that he has named a rough date for leaving my mind has decided to play the fool and convince me that I may be starting to like him again. Still not fancy let me point out, but like, maybe…

Anyway I had a nice tour of the ark which lead on to a couple of afternoon shandie's on the marina where another American captain (all be him older) was also chilling with a beer.

Unfortunately he was another irritating sort, yep, another know it all. But fuck it as it got quite entertaining for a while as the two Yanki captains were having a full blown cock off, young captain against old. It was interesting to see Tim get so irate and he also turned out to be a sore loser. Another unattractive quality to add to the list. Being as I was just the 'little woman', I was blatantly ignored. I was getting more and more annoyed with ship talk and needed to escape. I had taken just as much water going vessel chat as I could take for a day and made my excuses to head back home as I had quiz and bingo to get ready for.

After the quiz and a few more beers were consumed, the Yanki met me at my house and this is where the god awful snogging began. He is not a good kisser. Oh no. He kind of sticks his tongue in your mouth and then does not seem to know what to do with it once it's there. It really grosses me out but as I had consumed rather a few beers, I decided to just go with it and do the same so I also let my tongue lay flaccid too. Don't think he liked it too much, but come on! What did he expect me to do with it? Suck it or what? God I hate bad kissers...
Anyway, to put it in American terms, we made out, all be it bloody awfully, but we did it anyway.

Wednesday morning had me waking up to old flaccid tongue. With the cold light of day, he was definitely even less attractive. Thankfully he left soon thereafter. Alas, work had to be done and to be fair, I did it well. As well as one can when one's mind is elsewhere, thinking about awful flaccid tongues.
Anyway enough of that as ole flaccid tongue was coming over to give it another bash, this time with Pizza and DVDs. I was hoping he would bring with him some seriously hard core booze as I really couldn't face much more snogging stone cold sober. But as my luck would have it, no alcohol was brought and his pizza ended up as road kill on the way over. So as not to be rude I begrudgingly offered half of mine (that he had paid for). I am not a person that shares food, so this just added fuel to the fire. Why the hell am I still entertaining this man? Is it worth it seriously? God, I promise to be good from now on if you just let me out of this... Thank fuck that the DVD was good...

Gucci nearly went back to the pet shop after 6 years of togetherness as he tried to snatch a piece of my half of the pizza. Fucks sake Guch, how much more can one wannabe socialite be tested before snapping?
Anyway, I never did mind about the little things and the night was an OK

one apart from having to share my pizza and having to do something with that flaccid tongue again.

Even the snappy dressing ex suitor calling at 1am didn't tip me over the edge. I didn't answer in case you were wondering. Why is it that these lunatics think that they can get away with calling you all the names under the sun and then when *they* decide to ring, think that us Brits will come running?
In all fairness it is because some silly Brits here do go running. Notthisbrit.com

It is now Thursday and that can mean only one thing: Yes I have to bloody well sing tonight and as no one ever wants to get up and go first, that leaves me as the 'hostess with the mostess shitty voice' to do it.

Now where is my vodka?

Chapter 5 – August

1st August

Dear girl on a high,

With my blues well and truly gone, I have found myself wondering just what it is about periods that lock me in the labyrinth of doom. I mean we all have them, so that obviously means that I am not the only suicidal one out there. My mood swings may be worse than most because my spots clearly are, but what the fuck is it about a period that has you literally wanting to slit your own over emotional wrists? There should be a PMS group over here that one can just drop into when that urge of wanting to kill the closest male starts to surge through the veins. I may consider starting up one of those as a little money maker. Here in Marmaris I would make a frikkin' fortune because there are plenty of cheating Love Rats that can drive a woman into doing prison worthy crimes, and mix that in with the vile emotional state of a period, well, I would be onto a winner!

Anyway, after the Karaoke night had finished I nipped down to Faros Bar on the beachfront for 'just one drink' with my old friend Tuna (honest to god his name is Tuna) who was on holiday, you remember, the original snogging buddy. Just one drink turned into a bad assed night down Bar Street. I can't even say that I was dressed for the occasion, but at least I had my lashes on!
The night was a damn good one (?) however I have no idea how I got home or what time that may have been, but I do know one thing: Waking up on the hallway floor fully clothed with my handbag still on my shoulder

and my killer heels still attached to my feet means that I didn't make it up to bed. I thought for a moment that I may have pissed myself until I realized that there was an empty bottle of water in the general area of my crotch. I must admit that I smelt it just to make sure.

Once Gucci pissed on me and I thought it was my own all day long until I decided to smell his wee. I wondered how the hell it had got in my hair for fucks sake. I'm just lucky he didn't opt for a number two.

Sleeping on the hallway floor was a truly shit idea as now I am thoroughly aching all over and that does not do this nearly 31 year old body any good at all. Ahh well, at least my lashes were still intact. One was found attached to my forehead and the other on Gucci's nose.

Wouldn't you know it, Friday delivered a hangover to me with such force that I really was not able to do much apart from vegetate. I did manage to cook for the flaccid tongued Yanki though. What is it that they say; the way to a man's heart is through his stomach? Hope so! Why? Well dear diary, maybe it was more hormonal than reality that made my skin crawl. So, I am testing the waters yet again and hoping for the best. I think he enjoyed the meal as he went and helped himself to seconds. I was not offering seconds by the way as I wanted to freeze some for later in the week. The greedy bastard has annoyed me again! I'm thinking not hormonal and more reality after all... Anyway he stayed over and it was OK. Not good, not bad. One thing that I really didn't appreciate is when we went up to watch a bit of Lost in my bedroom, he proceeded to take his jeans off and I discovered that he was commando. He mentioned something about it being laundry day, whilst sitting on my bed, getting my clean sheets all caught up in the crack of his arse. Oh dear god I could have died. Honest to arse, he was lying there with his schlong hanging out, legs crossed, as if it was the most normal thing ever. I offered him some pants. He declined the offer with a shrug of the shoulders informing me that he liked to be naked. He may like it but believe me, I didn't! He raped my clean sheets FFS! Putitthefuckaway.com

Saturday morning could not come quickly enough. Thankfully Yanki and his schlong didn't hang around for long. So I went about my normal routine of watching the Eastenders omnibus. Two full hours of catch up definitely chilled me out; it was just what I needed to remove that grim image from my mind. Oh fuck it, now it's back again.

I actually had no plans to go out and party, and didn't even wish to go out which is rather odd to say the least. I decided to go for a catch up with Lorraine to pass a couple of afternoon hours instead. What is it about two fully grown adult women and their need to talk for hours without coming up for breath? The Yanki's arse crack and schlong were discussed in detail with venom. Having your girlfriends and Mingers around you is the only way that you can survive in this crazy land I swear. Roll on the winter when I can be on constant catch up with my friends!

Kaan was not hitting the town either so we decided to have an 'Amy Winehouse' remembrance night round at my house. No kissing in sight as funnily enough my mind was on the Yanki. Not his nasty schlong, just him. WTF is it about this bloody silly flaccid tongued Yanki??????

Sunday came and so did the Yanki. He came to pick me up in true white knight style on a scooter and off we went, up the mountains for a make shift picnic. We had a wicked day and I got my vampire white skin burnt to buggery.

Note to remember: He can be less irritating and more kinda cool while being drowned out by the noise of the scooter.

Anyway, to chill the skin down, a few beers were indulged on the marina whilst the Yanki [tried] to teach me Chess. I had an advantage as a little old British man came to my aid and I managed to win a game! I think the little old man was a bit of a dude if truth be told. He was not having any of Yanki's know it all antics and put him right in his place when he started to say that Chess is only for the highly intelligent. What the hell am I then? Chopped liver? Mother Fucking Yanki.

I also found out just how creepy it can be having a blog on the internet. As you know, the Yanki found my blog, but what he had failed to tell me previously was that his friends in America were checking out Marmaris online and happened to come across my blog to which they sent him the link. So his friends were reading all about my life and thought that I would be a great set up for their friend? Just goes to show that clearly his friends hate me.

Universe if that's you working your magic again, I think you delivered me a dud. I asked for a man that could kiss well and that would make me swoon. Instead I got flaccid tongued Tim, the clean sheet raping Yanki...

Moving on, Sister decided to grace us with his presence for an hour. By this time, I must say I did not wish to drink any more beer and after food and a chat with Sister, the Yanki and I went back up home to my house. He was clearly settling in for more arse cracking Lost, but I was having none of it and made him keep his pants on. I mean come on, who wants to see that dirty ole schlong?

4th August

Dear ranting loony,

What is it about freaks and weirdo's that I seem to attract? This week has
seen them all crawling back out of the woodwork and its starting to irritate
me no end. They seem to think that they can just wheedle their way back in
with very little effort other than incessant texts, Facebook messages and late
night phone calls.

Firstly the ex has started back up again with ridiculous texts. Actually this
one is a bit my fault as when I had check my dialled numbers, I seem to
have drunk dialled him at 03.55am. But he didn't have to plague me with
texts through the following day did he!?! I have no idea why I called him, I
don't want to know, I just wish I hadn't.

The next fool to start crawling is Mr. Attitude from Istanbul. I have not
answered a call since the day he got back on the flight in April yet he
continues to bother me with his pointless self appreciation letting me know
just how buff and toned he is. Come on, if he thinks that I am that shallow
to reply due to him being all buff and toned, then this tit never knew me at
all.

And today, the ex suitor. He has called, text and is now flooding me with
Facbook messages telling me just how much he misses me.
Urm, yes please, I am just going to jump back into the arms of each one of
these idiots.
Not.
Can they seriously not see that I am not the usual tourist that visits
Marmaris and that if they seriously wanted to achieve something other than
a lot of humiliation, they need to choose different tactics as their usual shit
is clearly not working for them in this instance.
I really know how to pick em don't I. Damn these ridiculous human
beings, and damn me for fancying them! Remember your mantra Lei: I
am an independent free spirit and do not need a man. It would be bloody
nice to have one, but not the wrong one. I'm not slating the females out
here that engorge Marmaris every year due to believing they have found

true love. I'm not slating them at all when I say bollocks to that. The sad thing about it is that I am under no illusions that even though the three men in question happen to be disturbing me, they are also probably disturbing 5 other females each in the hopes that one will fall for the shit that they are spinning.

Good luck creepers, good luck…

And to add salt to the wound, the Yanki has informed me that he accidentally left my favourite piece of kitchen wear, my hip flask, up the mountain when we went picnicking. I loved the mother fucking hip flask.

8th Aug

Dear depressed self,

Welcome to my labyrinth of impending doom. Yes again. I should know by now what to expect after a night on the town, alas, I never do learn. Indeed I have alcohol depression at its greatest.
Put it this way: Bugger all exciting has happened in my life recently. I'm nearly 31, my hangovers last for 2 days, I swear I'm putting on weight, men are just wankers and its time to trade in some of my friends.
Wannabe Socialite? Ha! If you bumped into me without noticing me, then I wouldn't blame you.

I need a break from this land, that's what I need. As it happens I have just booked myself a little holiday in October to visit the parents in Spain for a few weeks. They have lived over there for the last 10 years so I know the area well. The break may do me the world of good, or I may miss the Guch and become depressed as hell, but wither way, I will be getting outta here for a while. I may not come back. Wouldn't that be something? Viva Espania!

To make matters worse, this week has been dull and mundane to say the least. Tuesday was the only good one as I went over to the dark side in Icmeler to visit Minger Camilla. Dinner, gossip, wine, gossip, wine, wine, wine is how our night went. I love going to Camilla's house. It's like going home. I don't have to do anything, I can act like a stroppy teenager, I can drink without being judged and I generally just like it. In fact, thinking about it now, I should go up there more often or at least when I am suffering from doom as I get well looked after. Fair play.

I am one of these people that need stimulation constantly as my mind hates sitting idle. When it sits idle I start to obsess about whichever bloke I'm dating and that can turn me off the man or it can turn me into a raving loony. I have had to come up with a system for when this happens, so guess what I do when I'm bored these days? I build websites for fun and stock pile them. I don't even use them for fucks sake.

You can get stuck in a rut of going out and partying constantly (done that) or go the other way entirely and not go out at all. I seem to be in the middle these days, but I am not enjoying going out here at the moment. Therein lies the problem.

Hence the increasing urge to get the hell outta here and find myself again.

That flaccid tongued Yanki pointed out that I seem to be displaying rather a lot of self destructive behaviour recently. He is wrong as I am simply bored and do things to entertain myself that normal people simply wouldn't do. Maybe I am odd, but each weirdo to their own.

Wednesday was OK. I had pizza, I walked and I slept. The Yanki was present.

Thursday was crap on a stick, as was Friday.

Thank god I was saved by my Tunisian friend Chokri on Saturday. I have known Chokri for what seems like forever. We used to be cute young reps together in a past life and god the stories that we could tell. He is like a big gay Tunisian brother to me. We love each other dearly, but can also hate each other viciously. He knows each and every one of my buttons to push to tip me over the edge, but thankfully he decided not do that on this occasion. In fact we had a lovely night. We went for dinner along the beachfront, watched gay boys rip each other to pieces in Cheers bar, hit bar street, found the Yanki and his odd bud, went to visit Jess on her boyfriends boat (they are back together again), I passed out, woke up no Yanki, Jess and the boyfriend had an argument, we walked to Jess's house, I then decided walk another 3 miles home getting accosted the whole way, got home at 7am alone and welcomed the monster of
the labyrinth of impending doom.
I also decided to abuse my phone for a while. Always the best idea possible when in the labyrinth. Not.
A few people got hit with the shit stick but none were playing. Didn't they realize that I was bored and needed entertainment?

And the Yanki and I seem to have fallen out. Why? Cos I thought it was a bit rude to have dumped me whilst passed out on Jess's boyfriend's boat (apparently Jess had insisted for him to leave me there). Still, I have my opinion.

What a change a week can make eh? This time last week I was out picnicking and generally having a good time. Where am I now? Home alone with my foggy mist surrounding me.
Shall I just put on a bit of Adele to really push me over the edge?

12ᵗʰ Aug

Dear normal me,

As you can see, Adele and her dulcet slit your wrist tunes haven't pushed me over the edge just yet. Good job really as I wouldn't have wanted to miss this week's randomness that is my life.
After I finished feeling damn sorry for myself on Sunday I actually managed to drag up the energy to go visit Jess who was also suffering on the sofa, refusing to drag her sorry arse to work. We moaned a bit about life in general and then after much persuasion by me, we even went for a Sunday roast. It wasn't the best day on the planet, but it wasn't as bad as I originally thought it was going to be either.

Being one part of team Minger is a bonus as everyone that's in team Minger knows that if one Minger is down, they have to do their utmost to bring said Minger back on form, or to at least to the stage where one can see the light through the foggy mist. So Jess and I managed to bring each other back on top again. Go Team Minger!

Anyway, the start of the week was much the same as any other, getting over the mingingness that is the two day hangover. Sometimes I wonder how I can still peruse vodka when I have a hangover, but I believe a hangover is like child birth - We forget the pain, otherwise why would we do it again and again and again and again. Please note that I have not given birth, although I do try to convince Sister that Gucci came out of my flange.

I didn't do much apart from hate myself inwardly, but I manned up, pulled through and managed to not drown myself in a fishbowl.
Bravo me!!!

Tuesday was brighter. Put it this way, it came and went with the Yanki taking me out for dinner to pay me back for losing my dearest hip flask. We managed to argue our way through most of dinner about really ridiculous things, but hey, what's a dinner without an argument of some sort these days. He came back to mine and I proceeded to treat him to

watching a bit of Lost. Not arse crack Lost, just Lost.
God my life is just amazing isn't it?

Wednesday was a foul day. I went to the hairdressers to get the roots done
and came out with severely short hair. Not the snappy dressing ex suitors
hairdressers for obvious reasons, however it could quite easily have been a
friend of his considering the state of my hair now. Damn Turkish
hairdressers and their lack of listening skills!

Chokri my Tunisian friend was with me for the whole ordeal but that didn't
make the situation any better. We were due to be going straight out to
dinner after the hairdressers, but as my luck would have it, my hair looked
that disgustingly vile that I couldn't embarrass myself in public, so we came
back to my house instead and I cooked. That's another hairdresser on the
list to never to return to again. Although I was traumatized we managed to
have a nice night watching love films. Why is it that when watching
something lovely like a love I feel depressed instead of warm and fuzzy?

Thursday. Well what can I say about Thursday that won't get me into any
trouble? It was the most random day known to man. I started out the day
with the mission of going on the fake hair hunt. I just couldn't cope with
the shit on my head any longer and like the classy wannabe socialite that
am, I took myself off to the market to get some market hair. After
acquiring my gross market hair, I headed over to Jess the Minger who
was perched at the end of the bar in the hotel where she works. There was
a random customer also there that we now know fondly as Carol the crank.
We got talking and it turns out that other than being a crank, Carol also
claims to be a medium and that I had my channels open as all sorts of dead
spirits came to visit me. Hi dead Uncle in South Africa. Apparently some
dude called Paul is going to be very significant in my life and I am moving
to bloody Zimbabwe???? I do hope not.
Anyway, voices told Carol the crank to lend me her very
expensive sapphire necklace to give me protection and positivity for the
next two weeks. She said that if I am not feeling better and more positive
by the time she leaves, I am to keep the necklace until we meet again.
Knowing my luck the bloody amulet will choke me in my sleep.

After bypassing food shopping like I had done for days and coming home to a house where the fridge and cupboards were and still are bear, Jess called me up and informed me that we were going out and getting on it. OK I said, obviously. What sort of Minger would I be otherwise?

To keep the night cheap, I bought a bottle of vodka and took it back down to the hotel. I would have usually used my hip flask for vodka camouflage but couldn't due to fuck face Yanki.

Carol the crank was on the beer and on form with the channelling of the dead once more, so needless to say, I took full advantage and started asking questions about life, love and career.

Apparently I am going to be uber successful but still in sodding Zimbabwe. Piss off with yourself Carol.

During the 'cranking hour' we were sneakily slugging back the vodka like there was no tomorrow and when I eventually convinced Jess to leave the hotel it was 1.30am. The thought of going home didn't enter any of our heads, so we hit the beach front for some action, and action is what we got. The gay boys in Cheers bar were on it again hating on each other in there 'who looks the hottest in there tight white vests' way that they seem to bum off.

We moved onto Albatross bar where I was happy to find the nice gay boys that I love dearly and that always complement me on my choice of outfits. Some queens really are nice.

This is when you could have knocked me down with a feather.

I was recognized. Yes, me! I was recognized by two lovely young ladies that were on holiday (that do not know me from Adam) but are readers of my blog!!!!!!

Shock engulfed me, and I may have repeated myself with 'I just can't believe you read my blog' a few times. Still, I just can't believe that they actually read it!!!

After the thrill of meeting actual readers, we decided to go for some much needed drunk food. More randomness occurred. Jess being her usually self got talking to two blokes that joined our table. We ended up buying another bottle and drinking it all together on the beach watching the sun rise like a group of tits. The things you do when drunk eh? I was invited out to dinner by one of them, however I'm not really sure why as I was downright rude to him if I'm being totally honest here.

He must have liked it. I doubt I would recognize him again if I fell over him so that counts dinner out.

Anyway, another 7am in the morning job arriving home, alone, rather drunk and in need of some Gucci snuggles.
I love my dog when I'm pissed. He gives the best Mummy cuddles.

And then came Friday... Hangover and work is never clever. I had a meeting to get myself over to and I was not looking forward to schmoozing. However the universe was looking out for me as the two blokes that I was schmoozing with were fit fit fit!!!!! God damn I could hardly get the words out of my mouth with all the slavering I was doing. I was invited out to party with them Istanbul style (but in Marmaris). They are only here till Sunday and then back to Istanbul, so at the moment I am still deliberating on whether to go out with them tomorrow night.
I should just do it as they seem really nice and the hotness is an added bonus.

Anyway enough drivel from me about hot dudes as its Friday night and I'm home alone again. Seriously, I'm supposed to be a wannabe socialite not a sad looser that is home alone on a Friday night.
Looserville.com

P.S The fit French dude from when Nigel was here on holiday has informed me that I am very much welcome to go visit him for a long weekend. Hmm, France is so close to Spain and guess where I am going in October?
Look who's happy now? Must be the sapphire amulet that is swinging around my positive neck. Maybe Carol the crank isn't such a crank after all?

Adele? Back off bitch, you're not needed this week!

18th August

Dear pit of self despair,

Tonight I sent an email to the universe asking for some direction in life. It's not the first time that I have done this. The last time worked out so well that I was inspired to build my business, so you see, not all hope is lost (yet)... I suppose I need to listen hard for my reply, I know it will come, but I doubt in the form of a reply email cos that would just be frikkin' freaky!

Anyway, back to my week. After staying home and blogging last Friday night, I also decided to stay home on Saturday night too. I just could not find the will or energy needed in the whole getting ready process of hair and makeup. Men are so lucky. They can just throw on a pair of shorts/jeans/pants, a shirt or t shirt, squirt the aftershave and leave the house. They may not look great all the time but at least they look passable. I on the other hand, look like the bride of Frankenstein if I attempt to leave the house without having at least 5 changes of wardrobe, make up done and re done due to me buggering up my feline flick, hair done this way then that way, and then one more change of wardrobe so that I can honestly say that I feel less frump like and more mysterious vamp. Who the hell am I kidding, I look like exactly this when I go out: an aging wannabe socialite. I have also noticed that I am starting to get crow's feet around my eyes when I smile. It's OK, I'm making a mends with it. Why is it that we become so obsessed in looking our very best? You never know who you may happen to meet, that's why, and at the end of the day I am looking for 'the one' after all. I couldn't possibly go out looking un polished as 'the one' may look at me and then immediately look elsewhere, and who could blame him if I'm looking like a bag of turds. So, I shall continue with my two hours worth of getting ready whenever I can next muster up the will to do it (until I'm married that is, then I will get good and fat and just enjoy the hell out of it).

The reason I was in such an odd mood was because it was the anniversary of my dear departed Grandmother's passing. Don't get me wrong, she had a great life and passed at 101 years old this time last year. Her funeral happened to be on my 30th birthday, I kid you friggin' not. It really does only happen to me… That was a weird experience let me tell you. I hadn't seen a lot of my family for years, so it was great to see them on my 30th, however those fuckers wouldn't have come to my actual 30th had it not have been due to the funeral.

Anyway, I had the urge to get drunk on Saturday, so I invited the Yanki round on the understanding that he bring with him mucho beer. I barely managed to get tipsy. It was same old same old as ole flaccid tongued Yanki was more interested in talking about his day and what he had been up to. I'm getting bored of his shit now. Just for once I wanted to have some 'let's talk about my shit', but did I get it? Hell no. Even when I tried to bring the conversation over to me, he managed to wheedle himself into it somewhere and it was back to his crap boring bull shit. It's time for this dude to be put in a box and drowned in a river. Why the god damn hell am I wasting time on this guy FFS? I only have a few months left of the summer to find Mr. Right and get him to put a ring on it, so flaccid Yanki, it's about time you pissed off. I'm crap at dumping boys, so put me outta my misery and just dump my arse. It's not that hard to do, you know I'm gonna let you off easy with it.

Sunday was a right off. I managed to get my arse out of my self pity for a few hours and headed down to the beach for a much needed girly gossip with friends. It lightened the day.

Monday came and went with only one decision being made: I was hitting the town on Tuesday night. So I did. I was getting chatted up by a really rank dude so I called the Yanki to come rescue me. He happened to be in bed and after much persuasion he got up and came to Cheers bar. The problem was that the guy had left at the same time the Yanki walked in. He was not happy and is still not happy. He turned around and walked straight back out. Can't blame him really as he was in bed but well done to him for getting up though eh! Wanker?

Anyway my night continued with a bit more vodka, but I felt weird, so decided to take myself off home and abuse my phone instead. That was clearly one of the best ideas that I have ever had. Not.
I am still cringing at the messages sent and the phone calls made. Yes the ex got hit with the shit stick once again. Seriously, why do I do it to myself?

Wednesday was an odd day. My days seem to be getting odder and odder. I find myself with a large amount of time on my hands and usually, to a normal person this would be great as you could go to the beach, go swimming, etc. But being a vampire I find it hard to go out in the sun. So where does this leave me? Bored and indoors. Winter is great as I can catch up with all my friends as no one is working and generally there is never a dull moment, but summer? Well, not much going on really as everyone is working. And the pisser of this is that I severely hate being bored. Angry Birds works a charm for seven minutes.

I managed to go to the Supermarket. That was the extent of my day apart from getting a serious headache.

Today brings us up to Thursday. I actually did something today! I went to visit Jess and Carol the crank at the hotel for a few hours. I had to return the amulet that she had lent to me as it had started to give me a rash. Honest to god, her positive vibes amulet hates me.

Once home, after the Yanki had been ignoring me since Tuesday night, we chatted on Facebook for a while. I got dumped – Fucking finally!!!!! I feel my theme tune coming back "Another one bites the dust".

Oh joy of bloody joys, I can start living again ;) Why the hell didn't I dump ole flaccid tongue first I will never know. I could have got rid of him and his schlong a long time ago had I of bit the bullet. And he had the cheek to say what we were doing was 'Playing house'! No fuck face, I was living my daily life and you were along for the ride. Wanker tit fucker.

Apparently I am the most self centred person in the world when I'm drunk (said the Yanki tit, but I don't believe him). I would have said a bit of a small handful and occasionally irritatingly stupid, but self centred? That one was a bit harsh.

It's not as if I have never seen video footage of myself rather intoxicated before. Sister does evil things and catches me on film occasionally. I didn't think I came across as self centred. A wanker maybe, but not self centred.

I don't wish to be rude about the Yanki as he was OK. But OK is not what I'm looking for, so I must say this; thanks Yanki, you did me a solid as I was to chicken shit to do it myself. America is not the best at everything like you would have everyone believe, its Football not Soccer, the countries in Great Britain are not states, and you still owe me a fucking hip flask.

I am like an elephant, I never forget. Actually that's debatable, I do forget lots of things, but choose to remember what's truly important and that happens to be my lost hip flask.

If someone asked me what I remembered most about dating the Yanki, my answer would be that he lost my hip flask.
Fond memories?
Yes, but of my fucking hip flask.

Anyway, I am going out this weekend. Oh yes, indeed I am. A friend from Rhodes is coming over (Big Dicky, no really his name is Richard so we all call him Dicky, and the big part come from the fact he is a gym obsessed meat suit) and it could end up being messy. I think Big Dicky may think that something is going to happen between us, but I don't really like big blokes. Not my cup of tea.

I have had to delete the Yanki's number as I couldn't bear to drunk stalk that flaccid tongued tit over the weekend. And let's face it; the possibility is quite high that I would. Not that I like him, but I wouldn't want him getting the wrong idea. It's a shame I have my ex's number memorized and no matter how drunk I get, I never forget that God damn number...

And to make matters seriously worse, in a week I will be 31. Yep, 31 and single. 31 and an old maid.
I feel Adele coming on tonight, I really do. If I had a violin, I would play it to myself.
Man alive, I hope the universe answers me quickly with some direction. I don't think I can handle much more boredom. I'm hoping I don't do a Britney and shave my head in a mental bloody breakdown. Seriously, it could happen.
Come on universe, any suggestions are welcome at this stage. The only thing I may turn my nose up at is knitting. I may be an old maid, but I'm not ancient. Yet. That's next week.

P.S I have just figured out why I am in an odd mood. My back has started to ache. Welcome to my time of month.

Period, you absolute bastard you.

22nd Aug

Dear Monday night madness,

It's Monday night and I'm in a rather good mood. As this is
a foreign feeling for a Monday, I thought I should make the most of it by
updating the ole diary.
Yes I have just been dumped, but why the hell not start my week like I
mean to go on, in a bloody good mood and writing about it.

Being dumped by the Yanki was possibly the best thing that could have
happened to me last week as it made way for bigger and quite possibly
better. Bigger being the most suitable word of choice in this circumstance
(and I don't mean in the way that you think I do, being the good girl that I
am occasionally). Yes it is quite sufficient to say that I have had a rather
large weekend with a rather large Big Dicky. I have enjoyed it immensely
and yes, as predicted, I consumed rather a lot of alcohol. We had to start
somewhere and Jess the minger's hotel seemed to be as good a place as any.
As the vodka is cheap and the talk was good, it made a good start to the
night. From there we hit the beachfront for some good old fashioned
cheesy music in Cheers bar and then onto some seedy and totally dingy bar
called VIP. What's VIP about my heels sticking to the floor I'll never
know… After all the alcohol was consumed, (and I do mean all the alcohol
in Marmaris) it was time to head home, but not to bed like any normal
person would have done at 6.30am. Ohhhh no. Firstly let me point out
that I completed my first mission of not undertaking in any drunk stalking
which is always good, but I managed to miss my Saturday morning
Eastenders omnibus which is always bad. However the reason for missing it
brings us back to the good again as Big Dicky and I were still awake and
chatting until 11.30am. If I could remember what on earth we chatted
about till that time I would jot it down, however being nearly 31, my nearly
31 year old mind has chosen to forget the details. It couldn't have been the
alcohol.

Yes, Friday was a good one.

After 2 hours sleep and waking up still rather intoxicated, the only thing for
it was to go out and consume a shandy or two over a late lunch with Jess
and Big Dicky whilst we decided upon the evening's activities.
Saturday night arrived and as I only had to top up on alcohol levels, it
wasn't long before that tipsy feeling crept over me. This time we hit bar
street in style. Another good night had by all. When I say all, I mean me.
I can't say if Big Dicky thought the same after leaving him in town as I
pulled my usual vanishing act, but all hail his memory for finding his way
back to mine via taxi. Not that he was invited I must add. He literally just
assumed he would be welcome. That was very presumptuous of him,
however I didn't mind. If I had, I simply would not have opened the door.
Good thing I was up and listening to tunes or he would have found himself
sitting in the doorway all night. He wouldn't have been the first... We
snogged a bit until he decided it was time to tell me something which I
really wish I could forget; if there is any way to put a gal like me off, he
managed to do it with one sentence. He told me he couldn't get it up. Yes,
you heard me right. The man can't get it up. He said that due to his steroid
taking to get to the huge meat suit size that he is, the steroids do something
to his little dicky. Seriously, am I being punished for something I have
done in a past life? Why is this happening to me? As you can imagine, I lost
my hard on immediately. He did attempt to make it up to me in other ways,
however it was simply too late. Every time I looked down and saw him I
cringed and nearly smothered the poor fucker.

Following that things started to go a bit downhill. I couldn't look him in
the eye. I couldn't laugh with him. I couldn't do much with him from that
point onwards. All hope was lost. Maybe I should rename this puppy the
flaccid one instead of the Yanki. Big Dicky clearly is not a suitable name
now is it.

If you ask me what my type is, I don't seem to have one. All the men that I
have ever dated are totally different in every way possible. It's not a bad
thing, but is it a good one? The Yanki spoke the same language as me,
however, in the grand scheme of things it turned out that he didn't really...
Big Dicky was alright until he told me about his penile problems. From
there I can't really see it going much further. Other than that, what the hell
is it with me picking up blokes that live nowhere near me? There is
the gorgeous French dude living in France, Mr. Attitude living in Istanbul

(still too close for my liking), the Yanki living on the ocean and now Big Dicky living in Rhodes... Is my sub conscious self trying to tell me something?

29th Aug

Dear birthday girl,

I am finally able to update after being hung-over for the last two days. Turning 31 on Friday is not what happened to take it out of me... No, what did it was continuing the party all day Saturday, Saturday night and then trying to on Sunday but failing miserably. Yes, us 31 year olds try. We may fail, but at least we try.

So my weekend kick started on Friday morning, the actual day of the turning of age, when I went to the port to pick up Big Dicky who had invited his damn self to join in the celebrations. I really did not want him here, but I couldn't be rude at the same time and tell him not to come when he seemed so eager. He had however brought with him near enough the whole contents of the British supermarket that he so luckily has over in Rhodes. Bless that limp Big Dicky. He also brought with him a new hip flask for me. That is seriously a bit cringe as he must have heard me muttering about missing my hip flask and then he goes and replaces it. Oh no, I just don't like that shit. It's totally OTT and must stop. He was starting to annoy me and be far too full on already...

As I had to work for the majority of the day, we didn't start the festivities until around 8pm. This is where it all went Pete Tong.
We went to Jess's and got straight on the Absolute. Not one of my greatest ideas let me tell you, especially as the ex text wishing me a happy birthday sending my head up my arse once again. Fucking bastard ex. He really is a shit. He doesn't want me but he doesn't want anyone else to have me, hence the reason he text me around about 10pm, knowing full well that I would be on the pop with my friends. Clever cunt.
My Absolute filled eyes can and always will see straight through him.
Yes I still think about him, but by god, I could never forgive him for what he did. I just wished I could remember that when I'm drunk. I never did get the whole sloppy seconds thing... Would I have him back? I'd like to say hell no. Notice how I said I'd like to say...?

Anyway, after the whole texting incident, we hit Bar Street. I wish I could say that I remembered it, but alas, I do not. The pictures have not even convinced me that I was there either. I do on the other hand have rather a lot of scratches and bruises that have been inflicted by a possibly rabid dog that I apparently would not leave for over an hour. The dog was not small. It was a guard dog that happened to be a bloody big German Sheppard that was on a chain, tied up due to it being so vicious. I off course thought that it would be a sweet thing if you were nice to it, but, as usual, I was wrong and have the scratches to prove it... This was all before getting to Bar Street!

I even bought a new dress for the occasion, but as I don't remember wearing it, I get to wear it again really soon. I seem to have lost the belt for it though...

Big Dicky stayed at mine, but thankfully I was too out of it to have to sit through another limp dick .

Anyway, that was Friday. Saturday I missed the Benders from Eastenders once again. I seriously need to learn a lesson here and stop drinking on a Friday night. Other than that, we all went out for lunch and didn't come home till 3am. Lunch turned into shandie's, shandie's turned into Beers, Beer's turned into Vodka's, and I turned into a some sort of wanker. Normal night out then...!

Sunday was a different . I tried to force a shandie down me but it was just not happening. I may have sulked for a while about this. Jess and Big Dicky on the other hand were not suffering at all and it seemed to be going down a treat for them, so why not for me? Alcohol poisoning probably. Anyway we did a few hours on the beach and then down to the marina for another hour until I could take the pain no longer and needed to get back to the comfort of my own home. I was greeted with a lovely surprise of the house looking like a bog. The damn house just seems to keep messing itself up...!

And then there was today. Day two of the stinking hangover. I have not felt the love one little bit today. Big Dicky has had to deal with vicious Lei for the last couple of days too. Unfortunately I could not hide my disgust for him any longer. Jess was trying to tell me to be nice, but I just couldn't manage it. He was being too nice to me and it was making me feel sick. I half put it down to that manipulative ex texting me. He turned my head inside out from the Friday night onwards. And off course the other half of it is that Big Dicky is too cringe for me.

And to top it all off, the stupid Yanki has blocked me from viewing his wall on facebook. So, nothing else for it but to delete that fucker.
Why he wanted to restrict my access is beyond me. It's not like I ever wanted to drunk stalk him.
Even though I now have a new hip flask, I still have not gotten over the loss of the first one. RIP my funky hip flask :(

The weekend is now over, but no time for the impending doom to set in as we are on it like a car bonnet tomorrow night for Bayram. Needless to say it will end in disaster as it always does. I think I will leave the phone at home as at least then I won't be tempted to bombard that looser ex with texts. Well, not until I get home anyway. The thing is the sucker always replies! What the hell is wrong with him? I pick fights for the fun of it and he replies. Without fail!

Watch this space?

31ˢᵗ Aug

'

Dear dirty secret keeping gal,

I have a secret. And a bloody big one it is too. I will come back to that shortly though as I need to tell you exactly how I came to have this dirty secret...

After dropping Big Dicky off at the port on Monday afternoon, Jess and I went to the beach for a few hours. As we got talking I asked about a guy that we simply refer to as the Player who I had one date with and decided that he was not for me. He happens to be Saffy the Minglet (Jess's daughter) boyfriend's brother. Why he is known as the Player is a bit of a joke really as he is the total opposite of just that. The reason I thought he was not for me is not that he is unattractive, because believe me he really is. It's just that he is 5 years younger than me, he seemed far too keen and he was just a bit full on. You know how I like them to be bastards and to make me do some of the leg work, well this guy didn't fit that bill. Anyway, when I asked about him, Jess told me that he has actually turned into a bit of a man about town and was dating around. He had grown into his name and this somehow sparked my interest. I may have got my hard on back that I thought had gone for good after Big Dicky.

After leaving the beach I decided to text the Player. He replied and we had a bit of too and fro texting about nothing important. I kept this to myself and didn't let on to Jess. As it was Bayram, I was guessing that he would be out on the town like the rest of us. So with my plan firmly in mind, we went out last night. Indeed Team Minger hit the town in style. As it turned out, everyone and their dead goat was in Bar Street and we had a damn good night. I met up with Jess at the marina to start the night off with cocktails. Although it wasn't planned, the Player came for a quick drink as Saffy's boyfriend had called him and told him we were all there. Still no one knew about the texting and certainly not of my plan, so it seemed to be working quite well. He only stayed for one drink as he was meeting up with his friends elsewhere.

It was that kind of night where the sun was glowing and slowly sinking behind the mountains, the tone of the music was shifting from relaxing, strolling along the marina tunes to faster beats and everyone was getting ready to flood into the craziness of bar street just like us. Team Minger ended up going to a few different bars in bar street, bumping into various people along the way including Kaan and a rather charismatic dentist that I took a shine too. As the night continued and I had quite a few drinks inside, I started to feel the need to go home. Also Jess and I had words and I didn't wish to be in her company anymore. Dam us drunk Mingers! On the way home I text the Player and invited him back to mine. Well bugger me, he jumped at the chance. But I needed to explain something to him first… When he finally arrived at my house, I sat him down and told him that I was not looking for a relationship (WTF??), what I was looking for was a friend with benefits. He argued a bit about this, but decided to go with the flow of what I was saying, and with that, benefits time was upon us.

Man alive can that boy kiss! I was in snogging heaven! He stayed until 7.30am when he had to leave to go to work and I fell into a satisfied sleep. I haven't told a soul about this and I have told him not to as well. It's kind of fun having a secret (and a friend with benefits). He text earlier and asked if he could come over tonight. I have agreed to this and he is coming over at 1am when he finishes work. Usually for me that's a bit on the late side and I would have said no as we know what it means when a man wants to come over at that time, but as I'm in it just for this reason so woohooo I guess?

It is now 11pm and I don't know if am going to manage to keep my eyes open till then, but I am a trier all said and done. I've never had a secret of this nature before and I'm happy that I have one now.

The next instalment should be an eye opener. Here's hoping anyway!

Chapter 6 – September

01st September

Dear deranged girl,

24 hours ago I was on top of the world. 24 little hours ago… Since then the worst has happened. I thought I could just have the Player as a friend with benefits. Turns out I may like him a bit more than I thought.

He did not come over last night. All I could assume was that he had decided to go out and get drunk instead of coming over to see me. Mother Fucker. He text me today asking me what I was up to. I told him working, and that was that, no further messages. After I finished work, I went down to the beach to see Jess, Saffy and her boyfriend (the Player's brother). Unfortunately I couldn't keep my secret to myself and blurted it out as soon as I sat my arse down. Why the hell couldn't I keep my secret? For God's sake, I wanted it on the Q-T for a reason, but my bloody mouth runs away with me when I am excited about something. After I had told them, they were in a slight state of shock but came round to the idea rather quickly. Jess even confided in me that he really likes me and is looking for a serious girlfriend. This put a smile on my face. That was until Saffy mentioned that her boyfriend had told her that he was seen in Bar Street last night with Russian girls… Well fuck me is all I have to say to that.

I text the Player and said very simply: You last night, bar street, Russian girl. I got a reply a few hours later asking how I knew about it. I'll give him this, he didn't even attempt to deny it! He asked if I had a problem him being with a Russian girl. I shouldn't, but I do. It was after all me that had told him we were just going to be friends with benefits. It was after all me that told him I wanted him for no other reason apart from the sex. So why do I feel wretched about it now then? Because I am a tit that's why. A big one at that.

The text I sent back was: Yes I have a problem. I'll not be seeing you again. No reply… Why is it that when you are sitting staring at your phone, willing it to light up, a text never ever appears. Bastard phone. Bastard Player more like it.

Damn me and my stupidity. Why oh why did I tell him I only wanted him for his sex? Did I think I was being clever? Did I think in my drunken haze that this would make me more attractive to him? I'll tell you what I thought: I watched a film on Tuesday afternoon about friends with benefits that fell in love, and I thought I'll get me one of them. I thought that if I found someone to become a friend with benefit's (which in itself is quite a hard task) then it would be all fairytale like and we would fall in love.

So I went out and got me one of those and got dumped for a Russian. Still no text by the way, in case you were wondering.

I received a Facebook message from the ex suitor Key twat today. Apparently he misses me. Why is beyond me. Maybe he hasn't pulled in a while… Needless to say I didn't reply.

Well, that's it now, they can all piss off. I am done for the time being. I can't cope with the male population any longer. I may do what I did last summer and have a man sabbatical. That's right; I was off men for the whole summer season. I did not have sex from May right the way through to October. I felt better for it let me tell you. It was kind of like finding myself again. I was me for a while. It was not that hard either after being dicked around by my ex for such a long time, I found it easy to be alone and to not want or need a man. It's really hard to explain, but I felt freer. The real me had returned. And when I knew that the one and only me was back again, I stopped the sabbatical.

Anyway, I have just checked my phone again which happens to be right in front of me and still no sodding text. I guess telling him that I would not be seeing him again has actually told him that I will not be seeing him again. In the back of my mind I thought a grand romantic gesture was on its way. There is still time tonight. He may turn up at my door. Or, and this one seems more probable, he will go out with the Russian that only wants one Vodka to get her into bed.

Bloody me and my watching of films that always have happy endings. Damn you world, this was supposed to be my final summer of singledom, this was the summer where I was going to find me a bloke and settle down. Damn it, this was the summer that I was going to have a ring put on it.

Now I want to text him. Should I text him? Will I tell him that I don't just want him for sex and that I think we should date? OMG I don't think I can handle the thoughts going round in my mind. I may have a glass of wine and see if that helps.

Maybe I will text the ex instead.

Damn you silly girl. Damn you! OK, I am just going to try to keep myself occupied enough to not text either of them.

I'm signing off and then chopping my fingers off.

2nd Sept

(14.45pm)

Dear girl that never listens,

I didn't chop my fingers off, nor did I listen to my own advice. By midnight I couldn't take it anymore and I cracked. I text the Player. I didn't say much, just that he was a shit and I hoped he enjoyed his night ahead with the Russian. I did not receive a reply.

I went to bed in a horrific mood but still hoped that a grand romantic gesture was on its way. At 03.00am Gucci started barking like no tomorrow and he only ever does that when there is someone at the door. I rushed downstairs to welcome in my grand romantic gesture, only to find it was the neighbours shifting furniture around. They do that in Turkey at God forsaken hours.

I did get a text from the Player today around 1.30pm. It simply said 'I am not your boyfriend'. No need to rub it in fucker… I didn't reply as I seriously have nothing to say to that. This was all caused by me and my big trap when I was drunk. As I hadn't replied with some witty remark, he must have got annoyed as he called me 45 minutes later and asked me what the hell was wrong with me. He went on and on about the fact that it was me that told him that we were sex friends only, it was me who didn't want him as a boyfriend, etc. I know all of the above is true, but it doesn't stop me feeling a little hurt about this whole stinking situation. I told him that when one gets a sex friend one does not need to go and sleep with everything else on the planet as one has a promise already. He didn't like that. I didn't like it either as I don't want him sleeping with the whole world then crawling back to me when he can't pull. Nope, that's not the way that this was supposed to work. It's just not how I saw it in my mind's eye…

So I sat and I mulled. What I decided upon doing was to send him a text. So I did. It went like this: 'I have changed my mind, I don't want a sex friend, I want a boyfriend. Take Care.' Read into that what you will. Do you think it says 'Sorry about my previous statements, you go and have sex with the world, whilst I find myself a nice reliable boyfriend'? Or does it say this 'I want you as a boyfriend, stop having sex with the world'? I did actually mean it to be read in one of two ways so that if he continues to have sex with everyone, then I have my back up by saying 'well that is what I sent him after all'. And if he suddenly does turn up with some sort of grand romantic gesture, I will welcome it gracefully, then sit the tit down and tell him what I really want…

As you can see, I am still waiting for a reply of some description. I could be waiting a long time by the looks of things.

Damn me and damn him!

(8.45pm)

Me again. Still no reply. I have started to obsess about the Player now. This is sooooo not a good thing. I need a distraction. Stat. I seem to remembering writing that once before? Ah yes, when I was obsessing about my kissing friend Kaan who also does not wish to know me at this present time… I text Kaan to come over for Vodka night for my distraction, however wouldn't you know it, he is taking his bloody significant other out for dinner.

I could do some work but I just can't be bothered. I would rather Facebook stalk the Player instead. Nothing has changed on his Facebooksince 5 hours ago. I unfriended him a long time ago, so now all I get to look at is total limited crap. Stupid limited visibility.

I have actually left the house today. I met up with Jess and Saffy and we went dress shopping as it is 18 year old Saffy's engagement party on the 24th Sept. That should be fun as they are planning on seating me next to the Player. How is it that an 18 year old kid gets engaged and then married before this 31 year old loser? I'll tell you why: because I really am a loser. I think I am emotionally damaged. Thanks ex. I think this because I can't flirt anymore, I shove a brick wall between me and any cutie around, and I have been told that I have fuck off written on my forehead. So what's a girl to do about this? Do you know what, I have absolutely no idea.

How does one stop being a bitch long enough to be nice and find a bloke? I may have to google that one as I'm drawing a blank. Why the hell am I obsessing about a guy that I dated once, didn't like, deleted from Facebook, stopped answering his calls and texts and then had sex with? I believe the reason to be is that he is now somewhat unobtainable. I always always do this. I always want what I can't have.

Let's have a little recap shall we:

My ex – Just wanted me for sex, then didn't want me at all.

Kaan – He is never going to leave his significant other.

The Yanki – Well, I liked him then I didn't, then I did again, then I didn't, then I got dumped.

Now the Player – He wanted me, I didn't, now I want him, and he doesn't.

of my life.

So where does this leave me? Home alone, with a box of wine, the internet and my phone. Oh dear God above help me now. This is going to be a long night.

(12.20am)

I'm back again, obsessing. I have managed to stay off the wine, but I'm finding it hard to control my insatiable urge to text him. What I want to say is this: 'I like you, I think we should talk'. Diary, I wish you could give me some advice on what I should do here. I want to know a simple yes or no as to whether I should text or not. I'm not asking the world, just a yes or a no.

Bloody hell, what to do, what to do!!!??? I have the devil sitting on one side telling me to do it and an angel sitting on the other side telling me not to, and then there is me in the middle thinking get a glass of wine and see how you feel after that.

Fuck it fuck it fuck it…

It's not like I haven't tried to occupy myself. I have painted my nails and toe nails in all the colours of the rainbow. I have been playing on google maps looking at my cousin's place in South Africa and I have been on Facebook for a while too. I have even smoked as many fags as I could to give my hands something to do instead of grabbing the phone and texting.

The problem I am facing is this:

-He may not text back.

-He may text back and tell me where to go.

Headuparse.com

The guy used to really like me, but I seem to have buggered it all up. I got drunk and had sex with him when I shouldn't have. I am silly.

My neighbour has just called me. I saw the phone flashing up and I nearly shit myself. He wanted to come round for a drink but I put him off. Once again, another guy that has shown interest but I just don't fancy him. I would get bored far too quickly with him and dump him, or be a complete cowardly bitch and get him to dump me... If I could only like nice dude's, alas, I can't. At 31 should I not have grown out of this shit by now?

A glass of wine seems to have appeared in my hand. I feel it is doing me the world of good because if I get pissed, I have an excuse for texting him.

Anyway, the diet pills I am on are not pleasant at all. If I have not documented my addiction to diet tablets previously, I must tell you this has been ongoing for the last 3 years or so. I have tried every pill known to man and I am now on the most evil ones ever. I may have lost 1 pound, but I have also gained some dodgy discharge. Yes, I have to admit, my anal passage is leaking vile orangy oil stuff. And if you fart you have the trauma of a possible follow through of oily discharge. Why am I still on them? I paid 100tl for them and that 100tl will not go to waste. Well, anal waste only...

To top off my night, Kimmy and I were supposed to be going to the curry house Taj Mahal for my birthday treat (we are obvs on speaking terms again), but she cancelled on me yesterday not stating a reason. I didn't think much of it as she is a busy girl at work, until I saw her status on Facebook tonight: 'Has enjoyed a lovely lasagne tonight with *Mary Ann Jessop*'.

Well bully for you whilst I am sitting here dripping orange oil out my arse! I have come to the decision that Kimmy is no longer part of team Minger and she can piss off too.

Yep, so that's a man and a friend all in the space of 24 hours. Fuck my fucking life, seriously.

On the up side, I am going out tomorrow night. Could it be a disaster again? Who the hell knows, but I'm thinking that I should delete the Players number just in case…

(01.46am)

Yes I'm still here and now on the 2nd huge arsed glass of wine and I have text him. I hate myself already. What I sent was this: 'Hi. I want a real boyfriend not a sex friend. If you want this, we should talk'. It's been 5 minutes and no reply. I would really like a reply right now as I feel like a complete cock. I think this dude has actually got under my skin. This is a weird feeling. I'm not enjoying this one little bit. I like to know where I stand at all times and now that I don't and I have put myself right out there, it's a scary prospect and me no likey.

Ahh well bollox to it, if I don't get a reply, I will not stress about it. I will think of it as one of those times that one has put oneself out there in hope. I don't do it often after all. If I get a reply then bonus, if I don't, I will go with a theory that always works for me: 'it wasn't me'. I like that one a lot. The booze can take the brunt of it.

Still no text. It must have been a good 15 minutes by now. I shall finish my wine, go to bed and hopefully forget this ridiculous event has ever occured.

7th September

Dear tit,

A lot has happened since my mental breakdown. I doubt the Player will ever speak to me again, but I am totally OK with that as I have come to realize what a wanker he actually is. I never got a reply on Friday night, nor did I until the Saturday at 6.30pm. All he said was 'You don't know what you want'. And it was true.

I seem to had gotten very desperate over that arsehole for no apparent reason. But, I am glad to say that I am well and truly over that after what happened on the Saturday night…

Firstly let mention that I finally got up on Saturday morning to watch Eastenders. Yey me! I also managed to leave the house to buy myself a new top for the evening's shenanigans. I also bought a bottle of vodka for the very same reason.
Let me tell you about the vodka. It was cheap, nasty and messy. It was good. It had us leaving Jess the Mingers house in a bit of a drunken mess. Always good. We hit Buddha bar on Bar Street apparently. None of us have any recollection of being in there at all. The charismatic dentist from earlier in the week has since told me that I stuck my fingers in his mouth, claimed he was a vampire and told him to stay away from me and my friends as I knew what his game was.
Outstanding behaviour.
He has not taken offence and seems to have found it rather funny. I think I may have just found me a new date.

Dentist; A definite possibility.

We ended up back at Jess's house polishing off the last of the nasty vodka, until I turned into a psycho obsessive beast and forced Jess to give me the Players number so I could stalk the living crap out of him at 05.30am (I had deleted it before going out). Funnily enough he replied informing me that he was coming over to my house. This is when realization finally hit: He had never wanted me to be his girlfriend, he had only ever wanted me for sex.

Anyway, I sprinted home and he came round, bringing with him a friend…!?! I had never seen his friend before in my life and asked the Player why on earth he had brought him along. Neither of them had an answer so I threw them out. I kind of got the feeling that he thought I was going to shag him with his friend present, or worst still, he was going to ask his friend to join in. Out they went stiffies and all.

I followed up their departure with a load of abusive texts to which I got one reply: 'Sex'. To which he got one reply: 'Fuck right off'.

Sunday turned out to be a bloody good day. I woke up alive which is always good, went to pick up Jess so that we could indulge in shandie's and food, then more shandie's, then back to Jess's for even more shandie's. Hannah (Jess's sister) arrived with her brand new baby girl, the newest member of the Minger clan. God that child has got some lungs, and for a single wannabe socialite I can honestly say that could have possibly put me off having one for life. Cute as she may be, I am not sure how I would handle a baby. Do I think that I will ever have one? Really I am unsure as to that one, but I won't say never like I used to. I guess that must be my age showing…

I had a date to keep with Kimmy; yes she cancelled on me for a better offer but she rearranged and she was paying, so I made my excuses and left. Poor Kimmy, having me show up half cut… We had a great night none the less. Curry, Beer, good catch up session, what more can a girl ask for? Well, one could ask for more beer, and as I did ask for more beer, we went and met up with Jess and Hannah and had more beer.
Have I forgiven Kimmy for firstly not inviting me to her birthday party and secondly for cancelling on me for lasagne night with her work friend instead? Not entirely, but I'm getting there.

Yes, it's fair to say Sunday was a rather good day and night apart from the Player texting and calling as he wanted to know why I had told Jess that he had brought his friend around for a gang bang, but as I knew why he was calling, I didn't answer. He said that it simply wasn't true when Jess quizzed him about it. Not true my arse! Ohh such a liar but didn't want to look like a cunt in Jess's eyes…

I also made a bit of a decision and that is to piss off to South Africa for a while so I can get my life back on track. I seem to remember also deciding to go visit a friend in China too and Facebooking the world at 3am telling all and sundry that I am doing this. That went down like a lead balloon with the Mother let me tell you. She sent me a rather vicious email, but she does this about most of my status updates anyway so I take these things with a pinch of salt. I think it could have been the bit stating that I was going to blow all of my life savings that really wound her up, but I could be wrong...

Who knows what I will do, but I need to get myself a little look at the big wide world.

Anyway, I usually suffer from impending doom on a Monday night but I didn't funnily enough. The reason for this is possibly after I finished work I went and hung out with the Mingers and had fun, or it could be that I had been chatting online with the vampire dentist who has asked me out on a film date.

So this brings us up to date. Well, almost as the film date happened to be last night. And yes, I did go. As it was only a casual thing, I went in shorts and a casual top, but I did pop on my day lashes as I didn't want him to think that I am some sort of fugly duchess...

We chatted for ages, drank some beer and Raki, chatted more, he got his guitar out and I sang along to just about every song that I knew. Apparently Jumpin Jack Flash is a gas gas gas.

The film never materialized but what fun we had. He told me right off the bat that he didn't want anything serious, so this prompted me into telling him that I didn't fancy him anyway. I most certainly did, but I didn't wish to embarrass myself again after the singing fiasco. Anyway, as beer would have it, we ended up snogging for hours on his sofa and the snogging only stopped as I passed out on his bathroom floor during a wee break. Oh dear me... He told me today that he picked me up and popped me into his bed and he took the sofa. God love him. I would have preferred us both to have had the bed mind you.

He also told me that I am a damn good kisser. Well that's always nice to hear isn't it?

As it's nothing serious for him, I am not going to obsess at all. I only checked his Facbook page three times today so I am doing quite well so far.

He has told me how much fun he had and asked to do it again. A definite yes from me as the boy can kiss like a champ and he has this cool vibe going on that I am finding ridiculously attractive! I have in fact invited him to Saffy's engagement party and he has agreed. He then invited me to a gig on Monday night, to which I have agreed. So far so good. I think it's because he is 32 and has lived in London before so speaks perfect English that I like this guy.

So, to sum it all up, I am going to South Africa to sort my head out, I hate the Player and I have made a new kissing friend.

Life is good right now.

11ᵗʰ September

Dear oh so happy me,

After my wicked night on Tuesday with the Dentist, Wednesday didn't go well at all. The hangover followed me around for the entire day to the point of ridiculousness, so I took my self pitying butt up to bed early for a change.

Thursday was brighter. I did make a slight cock up though. I received a text message from the MOT people saying that I was overdue for my MOT. As I hate going to these places alone, I talked Jess and her hangover into coming with me. When we got there, I mentioned in passing that I hadn't even checked to see if the MOT was for Kastro (the car) or Betty (the scooter). I got the text message out and checked it properly. Off course it was for the damn scooter which had been so rudely stolen 2 months ago.
Duh...
So nothing else for it but to go back to Jess's for a cuppa and a fag before heading back to work.

The dentist was chatting away online and kind of invited himself over. I can't say that I was unhappy about that as even though he is a dentist, he is a funny one.
We managed to drink again, laugh again and engage in total snogathon again. I am staring to really like this dentist.

In the midst of all this the bloody Player called me. I believe it was 11.30pm. I answered the phone and asked him what he wanted. He said he wanted to talk, but that ship has sailed, I do not wish to talk to him ever again. Down went the phone.

I will have to see the Player at Saffy's engagement party but I'm sure he won't cause a scene whilst I have a ridiculously cool leather jacket wearing, floppy hair tossing plus one. Hopefully.

It was another good night with the Dentist which had him leaving my house at 12pm the next day ;) God alone knows what my neighbours must think! I have not seen him since but we have been chatting online trying to sort out another date night ☺

Anyhow, this brought us up to Friday when Jess and I decided we were not going out this weekend and to stay off the pop.
We decided to head down to the beach and have a thirst quenching shandy, and that's where things may have started to go wrong. I only stayed for the one shandy but it gave me the taste for it again. When I got home Jess called and somehow talked me into going out. Again. Well, what the hell do I have to loose, I am single after all? It doesn't take much talking into in all fairness. We are both pretty weak when it comes to going out.
So out we went. We hit Cheers bar and stayed there all night. We only managed to fall out once during the evening, but when we do fall out, there is a bit of shouting, then screaming, then comes the hugging and the 'But I do really love you my Minger'.
Pretty normal for us Mingers.

Kaan showed up with a girl who not his significant other. She was very leggy and all over him like a rash. This irritated me no end. He was not even hiding the fact that he was with her. She was looking at me like some sort of fool. She seemed to have pity in her eyes for me and I couldn't work out why. Kaan must have told her some bull shit about me before arriving... Nothappy.com

The vodka in that sodding Cheers bar must be the cheap crap as I woke up on the floor half in and half out of the kitchen fully clothed once again with my handbag still on my shoulder. I had one of my shoes still on, but to this day I have not been able to locate the other, it is not in this house that's for sure...
After peeling the top lid from the bottom, Jess called letting me know she was still a bit tipsy. I was too and it wasn't good. Food was needed immediately.
After throwing on some clothes I went to get in the car to collect the Minger but no sodding car in sight. I hate it when that happens as I am not a fan of public transport at all.
Anyway, as luck was on my side, whilst walking down the road in the general direction of the bus stop, there was a scooter heading toward me. I

flagged it down and asked if he wouldn't mind giving me a lift. He agreed I jumped on the back and away we went. Did I know this guy? No, but as it was broad daylight and I was still tipsy, concern left my mind and I was sure I wasn't going to be groped whilst on the back of the scooter. Thankfully I was right and he pleasantly dropped me off right at the Mingers door.
You have got to love the randomness of complete strangers in this country.

After nearly coughing up a lung whilst Jess and Saffy were in fits of laughter, we needed to locate Kastro who was found dumped near Cheers. It was time to feed the hangover, and then came the bloody shandie's. The shandie's turned into beers and we ended up back at Jess's house on the balcony playing with the dog whilst trying not to stalk people on Facebook.
And, as always, I decided it was the best idea ever to text the ex and say hi. The bugger answered immediately and suggested a few drinks. Being rather intoxicated I thought what a good idea. Fool.com. I met up with him at my house where I noticed that his hair has gotten more bit gimp like, I don't fancy him at all anymore and I think I have got to the stage where I can officially say I am over it and maybe we can be at least friends now. Have I said that before?
Good God did we did laugh... I don't think I have laughed that much with him for a long time. It was quite pleasant really but my mind was elsewhere. Thankfully he didn't try for a snog or anything else, but we did go up to my room and watch a bit of Lost where it seemed rather too easy to fall into our old comfortable TV watching position...

And now I find myself still alive on Sunday. I don't know how I am still alive but I won't be drinking again anytime soon and that's a promise. My hangover has not been a beast but it is present enough for me to say that I don't want to see it again for some time.

Jess has informed me that she didn't go to bed last night and as I couldn't be arsed to leave the house yet today, I have had none of the ever so intriguing updates as of yet.

I don't think my impending doom will be too severe tonight as I am going out for a big fat curry and catch up with Lorraine. Then I am putting myself on a sodding diet as I have eaten and drank far too much over the last week and it's about time that I was a bit nicer to my body.

12th Sept

Dear still slightly happy me,

Curry last night was a blast but I don't think I have felt so bloated in a long arsed time.

I have stopped with the nasty anal leakage diet tablets and gone back onto my old faithful tabs now. At least these buggers curb my cravings, however left me feeling like a baby whale washed up on the beach after dinner. All in the quest to be super slim to find the man of my dreams.

Anyway, when I got home and turned on the laptop, the dentist was online and we chatted away until 12.30am(ish). I was trying not to obsess about him, but I don't think I'm trying hard enough as I seem to have found myself severely obsessing over him. We just get on so well. I am going to go as far to say that we have most certainly clicked. What he thinks maybe a different but so far he seems as taken with me as I am with him. I am clearly not the best person to be judging his outlook, but I think things look good. He has not mentioned the gig for tonight, but he has mentioned cooking dinner for me, but as yet he has not been online to confirm this date. So I suppose I will just have to remain in limbo for the time being and maybe text him later to see what he is up to. When I mentioned that I was going to Spain for two weeks to visit the parents, he seemed rather interested in tagging along. This shocked me as it's my parents I'm going to visit after all, but the thought of having him there is making me smile. He was probably joking, so I need to get that idea out of my head unless he mentions it again.

13th September

Dear disillusioned girl,

Well the dentist actually did show up last night. It seemed to be going well at first as he brought along with him some beers and that's always a good start. We were chatting, laughing and snogging and it seemed that he was going to be staying over. That did not happen though and here is why:

1st point of pissing me off - When he arrived he didn't really looked dressed for a house date, so I asked why he was a bit dressed up. He said it was the gig tonight and that he was going along to it, but with no mention of me.

OK so he didn't actually end up going to it stating that he was having more fun with me in the house, but still, the intention was there to dump me and piss off to the gig, ALONE…

2nd point of pissing me off – He decided to talk about his ex girlfriend. In all honesty, it was me that opened the door to that one by asking about his ex as he doesn't like to talk about her at all. I wish I had never opened that flood gate as when it was opened he didn't shut up about her for an hour. He's not over her just yet then…

3rd point of pissing me off – This is the big one. The real doozy of the lot. My fault again as I seriously should not have let him have his way with me on the sofa, however I was caught up in the moment and I can't say anything else in my defence apart from the fact that I am the biggest tit I have ever known…

After the nookie and a post coital fag, he said that he was really tired and had to get up early for work so he was going home. I felt the wind knocked out of me because as soon as he said it I realized my cardinal mistake immediately. The reason he stayed over the last time was because I would not give up the nookie that night. Silly me gave it up in the early morning madness instead but that's not the point… So I went down the line of presuming that he would be staying over again. That will teach me not to presume.

Anyway, I couldn't keep the beast of rage inside and I let it out informing him I am not a 'sex and go' kind of gal and if he thinks of me like a fuck buddy then he could get the hell out of my house and never speak to me again. In his defence, he said he didn't think of me like that at all and most certainly didn't want to piss me off. He asked me what I wanted out of this 'so called relationship' to which I answered very diplomatically: 'I just want to see how it goes and take it from there'. Inside I was screaming: 'I WANT A FRIGGIN BOYFRIEND AND I WANT TO GET MARRIED!!!!!' But, that would have had him fleeing for the hills, so I kept that one to myself. When I asked him what he wanted, he actually said the same as me, which was surprising as I was expecting something totally different, so I suppose it's not all bad, right?

He then said that he wouldn't go home, that he would sleep over, but the damage had been done by this time and I was having none of it. Quite right too. So we half made up, snogged a bit more, then he left around 4.15am.

1st (and only) slip up on my part – I told him (after he had bleated on about his ex for an hour) that my ex had been around on Saturday night. He asked me what happened and I said nothing happened. I wasn't lying, but I failed to mention that he stayed over for the night as there is no need for that what so ever.

OK so maybe I shouldn't have told him about my ex at all, but he irritated me with the wowling on about his ex that I felt I had to level up somehow.

I made a vow this morning that I would not contact him first. As soon as I turned on the laptop, I could see him online, but I kept my restraint for once and didn't cave in. I guess you could say that I have won the first round, as he was the first to test the waters. Don't get me wrong, I am still annoyed and I won't be falling for the whole 'sex and go' thing again let me tell you, but I do really like him and want to see where this goes (if anywhere now)…

I will not invite him around, but he seems to do a good job of inviting himself. If he does not invite himself around, well, I will most certainly know why.

When the hell is my knight in shining armour going to show the hell up? When he does I am going to give him a piece of my mind for taking so damn long to get here and will probably end up scaring him off. Maybe there is a lesson to be learned in that statement.

I read something in a magazine once and I hope that it's true as I liked the sound of it so much: You have to kiss all the frogs before you eventually arrive in front of your Prince Charming. I have kissed my fair share of frogs this season alone so I must be getting close FFS.

Like I said, I hope that's true, but I do so like the dentist and wonder if we have both kissed enough frogs?

That, I am sure, will soon become very apparent…

19ᵗʰ Sept

Dear not so sure about life,

On Thursday I headed over to see Jess as Uncle John was arriving. Not my
Uncle John off course as I don't have one, Jess's Uncle John.
I really should have thought ahead and planned my outfit better rather than
just a t-shirt and a pair of shorts. I should have known that at 5pm we
would have been drinking beer and by 5.30pm, onto the Vodka's... Alas, I
didn't think ahead, and I was the only out of place person in Marmaris at
10pm in a restaurant looking like a tramp that had just been skipping.
Thankfully, by this time, I didn't really care.

Once the vodka was flowing freely, so was my urge to text the dentist. I
really should know better by now, but seriously, I don't. It was just a
simple text asking him what he was up to for the night. The answer was
not what I expected at all and put me in a foul mood when he said: 'I am
thinking of going out later, but you can come over until I go out if you like'.
Seriously, WTF! Off course I replied but unlike him, I was rather
diplomatic even though I was slightly tipsy: 'No thanks, me coming round
to yours before you go out does not work for me'. What a flaming dick.
The dentist I mean, not me for a change. I just couldn't believe it. He text
back saying that is not how he meant it, that he was going to watch a
Turkish band and didn't think that I would be interested, but I didn't reply.

I ended up at home at the decent hour of 11pm. As I had not had my fill
(and was still pretty pissed off in all fairness), I stopped by the shop
purchasing a couple of beers and decided to drink them whilst singing at
the top of my voice to 80s tunes on VH1, all alone like some sort of saddo.
I don't think the neighbours appreciated my vocal talents as
they rudely came and knocked on the door telling me to shut the hell up.
So, I opened up the laptop and the bloody dentist was online. He started
talking immediately asking me to come to the gig, but off course, no was
my answer. As if I am going to tolerate being an after though, I mean what
sort of woman does he think he's dealing with? After he had left the online
world and headed out into the real one, he proceeded to text me again
asking me to come to the gig.

At least he seemed to acknowledge what he had done wrong I suppose? My answer was still no. For one, I couldn't be arsed getting in the shower and getting myself ready, and for two, I was a bit too drunk to apply makeup. I would have gone out looking like some sort of clown, one lash stuck on my forehead and one on my eyebrow, and the feline flick – no need to attempt thinking how that would have turned out, and for a wannabe socialite that is so not a good look…

After he gave up, guess who started texting me? The bastard Player… I honestly did not text him first as I had deleted his number so it was a bit of a surprise when he text. He wanted to meet up for a chat on Saturday night. He wanted to seriously discuss the possibility of us being a couple. Urm, too little too late fucker! I told him I want nothing to do with him, but he didn't accept that. He wanted to come over and sort it all out, but I was not giving in, and eventually, he gave up too for the night…

So that left me with nothing else to do but to have a little chat with my Nan who passed away last year. I am not simple or anything, I was not just talking to thin air. Nope, my Nan lives in an Elephant that she bought in South Africa when visiting my parents that used to live there some time ago. And I know she lives in the Elephant as she likes to play little tricks on me while trying to freak me out.
I guess it did freak me out at first when she used to turn and face a different direction or be sitting in the middle of my coffee table when she actually lives above the fire place. But now it doesn't freak me out at all, I thinks it's great that she likes to say hi. My Mum thinks I play tricks on myself when I come home a bit tipsy, that I move Nan the Elephant in the hopes of tricking myself into believing its real in the morning. If that is true then I am a friggin' legend.

So yes, my Nan and I were sitting watching a bit of VH1 (after being told to shut up) and having a good old confab at the same time. It is fair to say that she squared me up.
Good old Nan eh.

I went to bed around 2am after crying my eyes out for no other reason than being a silly drunk female, feeling super clear about what needs to be done in life, and that meant going to bed instead of Facebook stalking.

Friday was a rather normal day. Not much else but work and chatting online with the dentist. Yes I chatted with him. He chatted first due to me still feeling slightly venomous. We chatted all night actually. It would have been a damn sight easier if I had just gone over to his house as he had suggested, but me being a stubborn bitch was not falling for that one. Anyway, I ended our night of chat by letting him know that he could take me out on Saturday. I didn't get told to go fuck myself or anything else, so it may have been received in the way that it was meant?

Saturday came with every intention to clean the house after the benders from Eastenders had been on, but that didn't happen.
Instead, I went down to visit Jess as more of her family had showed up for Saffy's engagement party. They all had raging hangovers by the pool, but not me... No, for once I was not in a cloudy state of affairs.
I didn't stay at the hotel too long, I got myself home to get ready for hitting the town. Even though the dentist had still not confirmed that we were going out, I had a feeling that he would. I was right. As soon as I signed online, he was there waiting for me. He asked if I would like to go to his house first for a drink or two then onto see his friends play a gig. I happily agreed.
When I arrived he had just got out of the shower and only had a towel around his lower half. Dear god, this boy looked good. A bit too good for a girl that has serious issues with her tummy. Off course I have seen him naked previously, but as I was not under the influence of alcohol at this present moment, I was a bit surprised at how damn fine this dentist was, dripping in water. I didn't rip his towel from his dripping body and make him take me right there and then, no, I kept my decorum, opened a beer and started having a hot flush that was rather embarrassing to say the least. As the dentist likes to drink Raki, he got his shot glass out and proceeded to get slightly drunk in a very short space of time, started snogging the life out of me and then invited me to go to Istanbul with him when I get back from Spain. Fuck me sideways!

We eventually made it out of the house to his friends gig. I was happily surprised to find that his friends were British blokes and what nice guys they were too. He then announced that we were going to Bar Street. He can't be ashamed to be seen out with me in public then! Good sign! It is fair to say that after a few beers, a few vodka's and then a few more beers, I was a little bit tipsy. [understatement.com] We piled back to Jake the guitar players pad where more drinking was done. When it was time to go home, the dentist wanted me to stay at his house, but I dare not leave Gucci on his own for that long, so I convinced him to come to mine instead. He did. We snogged some more and then went to bed ☺

Sunday was one of those cool, chilled out relaxing days spent on the sofa watching DVDs with my boyfriend the dentist. I felt filled with hope as he had given up his one day off to spend with me. Is this a sign that he likes me? I am still unsure on that one as throughout the course of the day he kept dropping silly statements into the air asking if I had fancied anyone last night, and when I said no off course not, he said it was fine if I did as I am a free agent. What on earth is this guy up to? He is playing tennis and it's getting slightly confusing…
Anyway, I dropped him off at his house at 7pm as he had a football match that he was desperate to watch, and I went back home with a slightly confused mind. Note to self: Do not obsess; let nature take its course.

This brings us up to today, Monday. Usually a day I despise, but it's not been too bad so far.
I have some old friends staying in Icmeler at the moment, so after work I went along to have a catch up session with them, did some shopping and then got myself back to where I am the most comfortable, on the sofa watching Lost with Guch.

The impending doom has not hit for a while which I find unsettling. Where is it, when is it coming back, do I want it back, do I even exist without it? Food for thought...

20th Sept

Dear impending doom,

Ahh there you are my old friend. I was foolish in thinking that you were not going to put in an appearance as you have certainly got me hung, drawn and quartered today.

My conundrum seems to be the dentist. But off course it is... I only chatted with him for 5 minutes online yesterday and not at all today, so what the hell is going on? He seems to have cooled right down since the weekend and I'm not really sure why. Maybe he has another woman on the go...

At least I'm going out tonight. Yes, it is a bit of a bonus as it will get me off line and looking less like a saddo. Maybe he can sit wondering where I am instead of the other way around for a change. I have no plans on telling him that I am going out or even making the first move in any kind of online chat, but knowing me I may cave.

It seems that Jess has also joined the gang of no self control as her and the ex (did I mention that they are off again) have been in talks all last week and he even showed up to visit Uncle John. She clams up and doesn't want to talk about any of it when asked, so I have decided that the best bet is to keep my trap shut and when she is ready to talk, I'm sure she will.

Anyway, that's me done for now. I really need to start thinking about cleaning this stinking pit of a house before the neighbours have rats to complain about too...

22nd Sept

(6.30pm)

Dear girl on a wire,

I deserve a pat on the back as when I went out on Tuesday night, I did not drunk stalk the dentist. Bravo Lei, bravo! There happens to be a reason for this though. The bloody Player was texting incessantly all night so he took up all my time. What is it they say about treat them mean, keep them keen? It certainly worked in this instance as I have been nothing but rude to the Player and the boy is not giving in. I wonder if that will work with the dentist as not much else is at the moment...

Actually he has invited me around to his house tonight, but I am in two minds whether or not to go. He needs a good old fashioned dose of obsession so I am trying to give him just that. Unfortunately for me I don't give it enough time for the obsession to be rooted as I can't stop myself from replying to his messages and accepting his offers to see him.

Why is it the ones that you don't want chase constantly and the ones you do know exactly how to play the game...

To make matters worse, Big Dicky from Rhodes is back. Not staying with me I might add, but he is here. He has got the picture now and knows that I don't want to get into anything with him, but what seems to be annoying me is that Jess and he are doing things together. He is even staying in the same hotel as her family and he doesn't even know them FFS! He has come over for Saffy the Minglet's engagement party on Saturday but I just don't want him there. When I think of him I feel my flesh crawling. He has done nothing wrong, this is all me, but I seriously do not wish to see him as I fear I may spew in his general direction.

The dentist is still supposedly attending the party with me. I say supposedly as he is that incredibly unpredictable that Christ alone knows if he will show or not. If he doesn't show then I am definitely calling it a day with him, nothing is more certain. I am feeling horrendously uncomfortable about the entire evening and really need him there to take my mind off the vile looks I will be getting from Big Dicky and the Player. I don't really need to say much more about this matter do I?

I think I have made the decision to go to the dentist's house later. God I am so easy.

(10pm)

I have not gone to the dentists, nor will I ever be going to the dentist's house ever again. I have deleted his number, all his texts, all my texts to him and the call log. Nothing else to delete in my phone. What could have possibly have happened in just a few small hours? A lot...

We were chatting online having a bit of banter (which is always good) when the convo turned to how he thinks women only want marriage and kids and how men get *'tricked'* into marriage. I told him that kids are not on my radar and they never have been, but you never know if you meet the right man. I asked him if he thought he would get married and he said no due to single being more fun. He was adamant that single is the only way he wishes to be. Rightio then. I told him I would not be coming over tonight as I do not wish to waste time on someone that wants to be single forever and how I want a man that actually wants to be in a relationship. He thought I was joking. No fucking joke king cock...

He told me to stop being ridiculous and to just come over to hang out. The answer was still no. We chatted for a while longer with me trying to explain why I didn't want to waste my time hanging out with him anymore, but he just didn't get it. The eternally single guy could not understand why the girl that wants a relationship does not want to hang out any more.

It's not as if he doesn't like me because he does. He tells me all the time when he's drunk. He tells me a whole hell of a lot when he is intoxicated. But when he's sober, he tells me he wants to be forever single. For fucks sake! What the hell is wrong with these men? I feel like getting a bottle of vodka, drinking the lot then going to hit him hard over the head with the empty bottle. I am now pissed off, very pissed off indeed. I am not so much hurt, but that is possibly because I was kind of expecting this, just pissed off. Don't forget he told me he wanted to come to Spain, he wanted to take me to Istanbul, etc. I think I could see through this at the time so I didn't let myself get too excited, but it hurts none the less.

Ah well, it was a nice dream while it lasted. Like always in dreams, you wake up.

So what have I done? I text the Player. I think it is because I need a bit of a confidence boost, I want to feel wanted. I text him a simple 'Hi'. I got the same right back. I am sure I will get more texts as I have opened the flood gates again, but I now need to figure out if I should really take this man sabbatical I was banging on about previously or if I should continue on my quest for true love... Clever people say that love finds you when you stop looking. Can someone please tell me how one can possibly stop looking when that's all this singleton really wants? This kissing frog's thing is fucking hard. Just when you think that you have found someone cool to roll with, the kissing is bloody marvellous and the sex is pretty damn erotic, something always has to fuck it all up. And that something is the dentist's will to remain single. I know that one day he won't feel like this, that his green light will eventually turn on, but for now I guess it's time for me to get my rod back out and go fishing. Crap on a stick, I bloody well hate going fishing.

On the upside, I have a Facebook friend coming over to Marmaris tomorrow afternoon. I have never met him before but he has been on my Facbook for a long arsed time and as he is slightly closer now than Istanbul, it seems normal for us to get a coffee and chat before he goes back. This is a strictly friends thing. He knows it, I know it. We have chatted about our issues with who we have been dating so many times before, so I am looking forward to boring him to death about the dentist tomorrow. It's always great to get a blokes opinion on things.

Anyway, I am once again left bloody dateless for the party on Saturday night. How sad can this get seriously? I think I always knew that I would be going solo. Fucking dentist. He did say from the start that he didn't want anything serious... Did I think I could change him? Yes. I really did.

27th Sept

Dear weekend of randomness,

This weekend has been seriously odd. Not just due to the fact that I severely missed the dentist, but in many other ways too.

My Facebook friend that came to visit was one of the oddities. When I picked him up from the bus station on Friday I was pleasantly surprised that he had his lip pierced and although not so much of a hottie, he *seemed* cool enough. It wasn't awkward in the slightest which was bloody marvellous. I took Mr. Piercing to a cheap bar on the beach front where we managed to chat for ages about nothing specific, have a few beers, chat some more and had a few laughs. It was clear to see from early on that this guy did not stop talking. It's not all that bad as it made for less awkward silences, but it's not all that good either…

After being suitably intoxicated we headed down to Jess's boyfriends boat. Oh yes, they are back together by the way. Notice a pattern forming? All Jess's family plus Big Dicky were on the boat. They had been out all day sunbathing and drinking and were all rather intoxicated. We got in on the action for a while before I managed to fall out with just about everyone. Why? Jess was really drunk and thought it would be a great idea to pick on Mr. Piercing for no apparent reason. We had a huge argument in front of everyone resulting with me stomping off the boat, Mr. Piercing in tow. Normal, but I was damn pissed off about it...

Still in my shorts and t-shirt that was now covered in beer, we headed for Bar Street. I had not a scrap of make up on but I doubt anyone would have noticed as the beer all over me made it look like I had pissed myself anyway... Not a proud moment.
Generally if going out at night (I have mentioned this before) I am a gal that will not leave the house without the hair, lashes, clothes and make up all in total perfection, but when beer happens, my judgment seems to get terribly clouded and I strutted down bar street thinking that I looked exactly like Claudia Schiffer. More like Marilyn Manson, without the makeup, when he first wakes up.

Yes, the photos show that it was not a pretty sight. Oh bollox, it's not as if I do it often.

After doing my usual disappearing act from some random club and wandering around for an hour in a bit of a daze trying to locate a taxi, a friend was driving past and offered me a lift and being the good soul that he is, dropped me off home. Funnily enough, on the way home we also found Mr. Piercing wandering around, so we picked him up too. Apparently I had left him in the club and done one.

When I checked my phone on Saturday morning I found some not so nice messages from him demanding that I collect him immediately. OK, the messages were a bit harsh, but possibly deserved in his situation considering he had never been to Marmaris before...

The rest of Saturday was frigging horrendous. I felt as if I my stomach was trying to escape through my eye balls. I couldn't eat, drink water, think or keep my eyes open or closed for any length of time. It's fair to say that my hangover was foul as foul can be.

I took Mr. Piercing into town for some food as the thought of cooking breakfast was making my stomach churn. Big mistake. I thought the pain I was suffering was possibly hunger; however after taking a bite of my sandwich it had me running to the toilet every 10 minutes for an hour to throw up. Better out than in? Then came the hot and cold white sweats, the dizziness, the severe head and stomach trauma and finally the need to go home and lie down for the rest of eternity.
The rest that I so desperately required was not allowed as it was the night of Saffy's engagement party. Oh fuckkkkkk oooooffffffffffff.

I was not sure if I was welcome after the arguments from the night before, so I dropped Jess a quick text asking if it was safe for us to come. I finally had a plus one, so although I didn't want to go, I didn't feel as bad about it as earlier. What I got back was something of a surprise. She said I was welcome but Mr. Piercing was not. When I asked why, she said that he had spoken rather rudely to Saffy's soon to be fiancée on the phone the night before. Urm, don't remember that one? Anyway, apparently no one wanted him there. Well if he wasn't welcome, then neither was I and I told her so. She said no bother and it was my choice. Too bloody right it was

my choice. I am no friend dumper that's for sure (I don't consider a
vanishing act dumping a friend). I text Saffy telling her why I wasn't going
to be there but she didn't understand saying that if a Facebook friend meant
more to me than her then fair enough. Point taken…

I was not going right up until 7.50pm. I was sitting downstairs in my PJs
still nursing my stinking hangover when a terrible feeling of guilt started to
creep over me. I didn't tell Mr. Piercing that he was not invited, I simply
said that I was going to get ready, go for half an hour then come back. So
far so good, he didn't question it. I got ready in record timing – 25
minutes. Put it this way, I didn't wash my hair or even put my face on
properly, but I was ready by 8.30pm to rock and roll, vowing not to drink.
I feared that I would be met with a frosty reception, but at least if I showed
my face no one could slag me off for not coming.

When I arrived, as feared, all eyes were on me. Fuckers. I sat down further
away from everyone else and when I was asked what I would like to drink,
before I could stop myself, a beer had been ordered and put down in front
of me. Oh what a bloody good move Lei... It certainly took the edge off
and for that I am glad.
When more of my friends started arriving (helping me to look less like a
leper), there was sodding Vodka's laid down in front of me. I am nothing
more than a pig and I know it. I started to feel a bit more at home and as
the night went on Jess came over and we chatted, Saffy told me how much
she appreciated me coming and Jess's family plus big Dicky looked less
frosty and more sunny with every sip of my drink.

The party was buzzing and most of my friends where in the same place for
once. Even the dreaded Player was not giving me a hard time. I think he
may have been trying to make me jealous by dancing with a girl in front of
me all night, but I could see right through that pile of stinking turds.

I had no intention of hitting Bar Street at the end of the party, but you
guessed it, I did. At least I had makeup on this time... The half an hour
curfew I had given myself had well and truly disappeared along with my
vow not to drink. Bar Street was not too bad at all. The only two issues I
had were Mr. Piercing texting me horrific messages demanding that I get
home in 20 minutes and the Player coming over to me and telling me never

to text him again. OK then nob jockey(s)… I must say I was not impressed with either, especially with the texts from Mr. Piercing. Maybe he was not as sweet as he seemed after all?

At least big Dicky and I had a good chat and he made me feel less guilty of giving him the crappy weekend he had the last time he visited. After I had done the usual disappearing act around 3.30am, I really don't know why but I think limp Dicky may have thought we still had something as he started texting asking to take me out to dinner the following night. Best not to reply me thinks.

I got home to find Mr. Piercing asleep in my bed. The bloody cheek of it! I jumped in as I was too tired to force him out. He was clearly not in a good mood, so I faked sleep and let him rant on to himself.

Sunday wasn't as bad as the sheer hell of Saturday. I even managed to get out of my pit, take the moody Mr. Piercing to Dominoes, hit the beach for an hour before heading to the DVD shop, and then home to have a marathon DVD session. Anything to drown out the crap that was coming out of his mouth.

Note to self: Do not invite another internet buddy to town. Each one of them has been a cunt to date. At one point I have to admit that I did feel a bit bad for Mr. Piercing. His trip to Marmaris has not been a fantastic one and I really should have showed him around some more, but when making nasty text messaging demands and being a general shit of a person, me, myself and I are simply not going to go out of our way to do nice things for such fuckers. I don't do demands, I never have, never will. There is nothing more certain that will put me off a bloke than nasty demands, so Mr. Piercing, as different as cute you are with your lip piercing; you are certainly not for me as a friend or anything else.
Thankfully he seemed to be in a slightly better mood by the end of the day, but believe me, I was glad to hear that he was going back to Istanbul the following morning.

Monday came with a bang. Work was manic and I needed to remove 'le freak' from town before any further damage was done. I thought I was in for a quiet night, however Jess reminded me that her family were leaving the day after and that we were all going to the marina for dinner and drinks.

Bloody hell, it never ends!

After dropping the misery that is Mr. Piercing at the bus station, I headed straight down to the marina to meet the fellowship of Mingers.
It was a good night, and due to me actually eating dinner whilst consuming beer, I did not get too outrageously drunk.
I still managed to be late getting home as we headed over to the boat for a few more drinks. Isn't that always the way?

So that just about rounds up my weekend of madness. I think I will try to stay away from alcohol for a while now. I feel I may be going a bit OTT at the moment.

28th Sept

Dear girl that actually likes the dentist,

I have been thinking about the sodding dentist again. Maybe I was a bit hasty dumping him as quickly as I did. Maybe after more than just 2 and half weeks of dating (honest to god that's all it was), this would start to become a tad more serious? Jesus, sometimes I really don't think these things through do I.

Kimmy realized I needed a pick me up and took me for brunch and a damn good talking too today. She indeed thinks I could have been too hasty with the dumping but also agrees that I should not contact him. If he decides to miss me, he is still on my Facebook, MSN and probably still has my number so he can easily get in touch with me, and that's all I have to say on this matter. Well, I have a lot more to say but don't wish to ramble on pointlessly about my foolishness. I mean, it's not as if I did anything really bad, I just told him what I wanted, found that he didn't want the same and nipped it in the bud right there and then before my heart gets ripped through the shredder once more. At the time I thought it was a good move, that I deserved better than what I was getting. Now I feel like a tit. This summer was supposed to be about finding the one, but what I have found instead is a torrent of twats. Can anyone really be so unlucky?

Unfortunately the good boys are just not for me. This leaves me in a bit of a conundrum on the man front. I want what I can't have. God damn it, why can't I be happy with a guy that likes me, wants to take me out, treats me right and is a Mothers dream? I just don't like guys like that you see. Stupid, silly girl…

Other than that I had a bit of a surprise tonight, the Yanki got in touch. Now we know that I deleted him from Facebook, however I didn't delete him from Gucci's Facebook as I needed him there for the stalker within. So, while on Gucci's Facebook tonight, the flaccid tongued Yanki started chatting away. I was pleasantly surprised and chatted back. That was until the 'know it all' started being a know it all and quoting my blog back to me about how unlucky I am in love and how sorry he was to hear about me and the dentist. Seriously, as if I needed to hear that and especially from him! Tit. I tell you what you can do with that comment Yanki, you can use your flaccid tongue to stick it up your chubby arse. With nothing to lose, I let rip. I told him exactly what I thought of him, he did the same back and now I find that he has sent me a friend request on my Facebook. What the actual fuck man? I am actually starting to think it must be me. How could it not be?

And with that, I'm finishing my fag and going to bloody bed with Guch for company until he farts me out again.

Standard.

Chapter 7 – October

3rd Oct

Dear poker within,

I caved in. As always. I couldn't help myself. On Thursday night I broke down and poked the dentist. Not poking in the literal sense, poking in the Facebook sense. This could have been a good or bad move; however it turned out to be a bit of a good one as when I signed onto MSN the following day, he pinged right up. We had a normal(ish) conversation and that's it. I continued on with my work and he probably continued to chat to all his other girls on MSN… No big deal right?

The day continued along as any normal Friday usually did. I was at a bit of a loose end and I hadn't heard from Jess, so was just coming to terms with having a boring night in when Kaan called and asked if I fancied vodka night. It's like he has physic ability's as he always seems to know just when I'm in need of a pick me up. I jumped at vodka night and 30 minutes later Kaan was at my house, vodka in hand. I remember chatting about his new mistress (booo hissssss), having a laugh and joke in general, but after that I draw a blank. So, I did what I always do, I called him and asked if we had fallen out. Apparently not at all, however he said I passed out on the sofa whilst he was in full swing of throwing up over the balcony all the while fully believing that there was a man in the garden watching at him at 04.30am.

I must have had a sleep walking session as I woke up in bed.

I won't be drinking Absolute vodka again as my hangover made me cry. Honest to god, it made me bloody weep. If I hadn't of already arranged to have X Factor night with Chokri I would not have left the house. Alas, I had made plans and I wasn't about to let that stinker of a hangover beat me. After contemplating getting my face on for over an hour, it got to the point that if I didn't do it then, I would have to go out without slap on, and that just wouldn't do.

Finally, I made it out. Tapping his foot in the campest way possible, Chokri was waiting impatiently to greet me with a look of sheer disgust on how I could have walked out the door looking like I did. Judgmental bloody bugger. I ordered alcohol. It was the only way to get through it. After several unkind words from Chokri about my choice of wardrobe, he eventually accepted the fact that I was not going to bite and he gave up when X Factor started.

During the course of the night, I got a text from an unknown number that could have only been the dentist as he is the only one that ever calls me 'dude'. He asked what I was up to and ask me to join him and his friend in Bar St later, to which I agreed. As Chokri didn't want to be seen with me looking the way I looked, he gracefully declined my invite and pissed off home leaving me with my stomach churning with nerves about the dentist.

I don't know what the hell I was worrying about as it was just as if I had seen him yesterday. He was his normal chatty and flirty self. I also liked his friend which always helps as I'm a bit of a weirdo when it comes to meeting friends of a guy that I like. I just don't know how to behave towards them. It's a tough one, seriously, because if you're friendly this could be misconstrued as being flirty, but if you're not you get deemed as the 'miserable girl' and the friend will talk the guy in question right out of dating you. So finding middle ground is of utmost importance. I opted for ever so slightly flirty and this leaded to poking fun at the dentist with the help of his friend. I think I got it right for once.

I got dragged around a few bars, the dentist all the while buying my drinks and me getting slightly more intoxicated with ever sip I took. We ended up in a club that I am not particularly fond of as the tunes can only be described as gangster rap. Have you ever seen a blond girl try to dance to gangster bloody rap? However, as my drinks were being purchased I had no real choice in the matter. I spotted one of my Turkish friends Ela. She is more of an acquaintance than a friend, but I knew her and wanted to look a bit popular so I dragged her over for a quick chat. Unfortunately this resulted in her parking her arse at our table and flirting with the dentist and his friend. Bitch. Thankfully after the dentist's initial flirty reaction towards her, he seemed to become enamoured with me and was trying his best to snog my face off, and yes, this was in public. Usually this would not be a problem, however my brick wall was still in place from our previous fling and it wasn't coming down just yet. I batted away his advances and gave him a cheek to kiss instead (and no it wasn't my arse cheek just yet) ☺ I am rather proud of this accomplishment, as it really was an accomplishment because all I wanted to do was snog him right back. Clever me though as this seemed to make him even more enamoured. I obviously hadn't planned it that way as I am not that clever when intoxicated, but it got a good reaction none the less.

The only thing that annoyed me about the night was Ela. Yep, she is a nightmare. A bloody flirty nightmare that never gives in. At one point she even asked me if my 'boyfriend' was gay as she was getting no attention from him. Jesus Christ girl, fuck offfffffffff! We ended up leaving her and the dentist's friend there and moved onto a quieter bar, downing a few more drinks then heading up to my house where we had a few more, and as I couldn't help myself, to bed we went. Bugger.

He didn't run for the hills in the morning. Nope, instead we watched films all day and generally chilled out until I dropped him off home around 8pm. I think it would be a rather safe bet to inform you that my obsession has returned with a vengeance.

Note to self: Please don't go psycho on his arse.

7th Oct

Dear wild horses,

What an odd few days... On Wednesday night the flaccid tongued Yanki showed up at my house at 7.30pm. It was a surprise to say the least. I answered the door to be greeted with wafts of beer tinged breath. Why he ended up on my bloody doorstep I have no idea but I couldn't just leave him there so I let him follow me in for a very quick chat. If I had thought that it was going to be weird chatting with him in person, I was pleasantly surprised to find that it wasn't, in fact there was no awkwardness at all. We were like two friends that had not seen each other in a while. Two friends that don't especially like each other much. I must admit that I relished telling him how the dentist and I had been seeing each other again. It didn't seem faze him. Dick. He stayed for a few hours, eventually pissing off around 11pm only to start chatting to me on Facebook when he got home. The conversation went something like this:

Yanki: I'm bored

Me: You have only just got home

Yanki: Yeah, but I'm bored. What are you doing?

Me: Much the same as when you left my house 10 minutes ago

Yanki: Shall I come over?

Me: Urmmmm...?

Yanki: I'm a bit horny

Me: TURNED FACEBOOK OFF AND WENT TO BED.

I woke up to a lovely message from him telling me that he was sorry if he had offended me, but if I was up for it, he would really like to come over and service me. How nice. I couldn't think of anything viler than letting his arse rape my sheets again or allowing him to stick that flaccid tongue in my mouth. I would literally be sick.

My day went about as usual, nothing exciting happened until 10pm when the dentist asked if I fancied going for a beer and to watch his British friend's band play a Jazz and Blues gig. Usually I would never accept an invitation at 10pm as by that time of night I am settled at home and wild horses can't drag me out. But, it wasn't wild horses asking, it was the dentist.

I am proud to say I got ready in amazing timing – 20 minutes! Thankfully I had already washed my week old minging hair earlier in the day and decided casual was the way forward and slung on a T-shirt, a pair of jeans and wedges. We had a nice time at the gig and I was surprised when Jake (dentist's friend) asked when I was going to Spain for my holidays. That meant that the dentist has spoken about me. Oh my fucking God, progress! I didn't go home. I went to the dentist's house and remained there until I woke up this morning with a great big bloody smile on my face. I am still wearing it now.

We have slid back into things pretty smoothly I would say. How long this is going to last I have no idea, but I am trying to go with the flow and doing a mighty fine job of it so far. I have not Facebook stalked him (much), I have not obsessed about him incessantly and I have not sent him messages. Well done that girl.

Anyway, enough for now as Kaan has called and suggested vodka night.

Well, it is Friday after all…

11th Oct

Dear dater chick,

Things seem to be looking up all round. I enjoyed vodka night with Kaan and there seems to be somewhat of a shift happening with the dentist. He is more chatty, seems to want to see me a lot more and well, I don't know, but somehow I think he is starting to see me as less of the casual kind of gal that maybe he saw me as before. I knew two weeks was a silly time frame to base my earlier meltdown on!

Let me explain… On Saturday night Chokri and I did the usual: Dinner, drinks, gossip and off course watching the X Factor. I had already half arranged to meet the dentist later, but as always things were not set in stone for what we were going to do. Once X Factor had finished I sent him a quick text asking what he was doing and we made arrangements to meet up in Bar Street. When we got down there we found the dentist alone. This is not unusual. He seemed to be in a bit of an odd mood, but again, this is also not unusual. We hit a bar that is always full of reps and ex-pats due to the cracking discount we get and the tunes are usually banging too, well, at least no effing Gangster Rap. A nice surprise was finding Kaan there, not so nice was that he had brought that pin-up mistress of his. For the first time ever I didn't feel sick at the sight of them. Must like this dentist then…

Everyone crowded around our table leaving me in my element and the dentist looking rather ill at ease. I introduced him to everyone and thought that he might perk up, but didn't. Chokri suggested that we go to another bar, just me and dentist, and even though I wanted to stay and show him off to my friends, I didn't. We ended up in the rock bar next door that was a firm favourite for both of us. He seemed to liven up as soon as we got through the door as he found some friends immediately. Funnily enough though, he didn't introduce me to them and only the ones I already knew were pleasant to me. Ignorant sods.

The night went on and eventually the dentist and I decided to head back to my house for a few more drinks. Although he may have been in an odd mood to start with we had a good night, and once again, he did not run for the hills on the Sunday morning. Instead, he asked for breakfast. Usually I am not a gal that gets up and cooks a man breakfast; however I quite fancied the idea of cooking this man his breakfast.

It was funny sitting down and eating with him on a Sunday morning in a rather sober state. I think I liked it. And after that we enjoyed a day on the sofa watching films and shagging. Yes it was a good Sunday.

Monday was the start of a new week and it is the week that I am going on my holidays to Spain. I didn't think that I would be seeing the dentist again before I went and it didn't worry me as I had been with him all weekend. I cracked on with work and doing a food shop for Saffy the Minglet who is Gucci sitting for me while I am on my jollies. Once I was back online, the dentist asked what I was making for dinner. I had thought about a tagliatelle with cheese sauce for myself until he announced that he didn't like cheese sauce and suggested spaghetti bolognaise instead. Urm, coming for dinner then are you dentist? Actually yes, he invited himself around for a spag bol. I didn't mind at all, in fact I really bummed of the fact that he wanted to come over for dinner. So I cooked up a vegetarian feast, even if I do say so myself.

We didn't do too much other than eat, watch a DVD and have Gucci's beady little eyes watching the dentist maul his Mum, willing him dead. It was a bloody marvellous night and it reminded me of what it's like to have a boyfriend. Jesus, I have not had one of those for some absurd amount of time and I hope to God that I don't fuck this one up… Not that he is my boyfriend. Not yet anyway…

He didn't stay over, but I really didn't mind. Too much of a good thing can make you sick, so I guess it was best all round that he took himself off home and left me with another huge smile glued to my face.

Note to self: Whilst on holiday visiting the parents, remember that one is on an eternal diet and one should not overindulge in Sunday Roasts and three course meals. The last time one did this one ended up a huge fatty and subsequently one is now addicted to diet pills. You have a deal to seal with the dentist and dentists don't like portly Brit's.

13th Oct

Dear fool that should not have got drunk the day before a horrific amount of travelling,

I went for dinner with Jess last night. I had not seen the Minger for a good two weeks and was desperate to tell her my updates and was dying to hear her's. We didn't half have a bloody good catch up! After dinner and copious amounts of Vodka, I thought it a good idea to text the dentist to see if he fancied a quick drink. The reply was a simply 'yes, come over'. Bless him, it was gone midnight already. I hot footed it over to his house where we drank beer, got a bit silly on vodka, and then passed out at stupid o clock in the morning.

I don't remember too much of the goings on, but I had a good feeling inside me when I left his house earlier, you know, one of those feelings where you can't stop the smile from creeping right across the face and people actually think you are some sort of deranged wanker. It didn't last long though as my hangover appeared far too quickly and I had far too much to do before heading for the airport at 12.30am. But, like the trooper that I am, I powered though, managing to chat to the dentist online in-between jobs. Saddo. Me, not the dentist.

I have now cleaned the house from top to bottom ready for Saffy to come Guch sit, I have done all the work that I can possibly do before setting off, I have made my sandwiches for the journey and, I have finally packed my suitcase. It is now 10pm and the hangover is at its worst, I am desperate to sleep, I feel terribly irritable, I don't want to leave Gucci (or the dentist) and I won't be getting to Spain until late tomorrow afternoon.

Damn me and my stupid ideas for having a few sodding drinks.

14th Oct

Dear girl on holiday,

I have arrived! Yes I am safe, sound and happy in Spain; however the
journey was a different story entirely.

It was a SHIT idea to get hammered the day before travelling, but it has
taught me a lesson. It's fair to say when I left the house on Thursday night
I really was not prepared for the long looooong assed journey ahead of me.
Seriouslytogod.com

Getting to Dalaman was easy enough. The flight to Istanbul was also plain
sailing. What was not so much plain sailing (more tearing my hair out in
sheer tiredness and frustration) was the 7 hour wait for my connecting
flight at Istanbul airport.
Yes that really did test me.
There was no where to park my ridiculously tired and hung-over arse and I
really was in no mood to go duty free shopping, so nothing else for it but to
sit on the floor. After being sat for 3 hours and pissing about on my lap
top as best I could with no wifi, I accidentally dropped to sleep. When I
woke up, rubbed my eyes and looked at my watch, panic surged through my
veins. I had overslept and only had 10 minutes to make it to my boarding
gate before it closed.
Did I have any idea where I was going? Off course not. But like the
determined gal that I am, I found my way running like a banshee on
steroids and upsetting a few unsuspecting people who managed to get in
the way of my mad dash.
As you can see though, I made it. Tiredness and all, I finally got into the
parents house at 5.30pm today.

On the up side, the weather is grey. I say upside as I am now so sick of the
hot sunny days that Marmaris brings that I thankfully welcome
this greyness with open arms.

I miss Gucci already. He was not a happy piglet when I left last night. But, as I have already been informed by Saffy, Gucci is as predicted getting spoilt rotten.

I have also managed to catch up with the dentist. He nearly said he missed me. Nearly… What he actually said was 'I'm not going out tonight, I'm going to bed alone for a wank cos you're not here'. Yes, nearly…

I think I have gone well and truly past the vile stage of tiredness and am now into the hallucination stage, so let me take this opportunity to let you know that if you don't hear from me for a while, the G and T in my hand may have something to do with the severe crash that I feel is soon to be upon me...
It truly was a fuck nut of a journey and now I need my pit. Bring on the 14 hours sleep I am about to fall into.

And with that, I bid you goodnight.

17th Oct

Dear Tourist from Turkey,

Day 4 already? Un-frikkin' believable! Time flies when you're having fun and that doesn't matter what country you happen to be in!

My mind is finally more Zen and I hadn't actually realised how much of a break from Marmaris I needed until I had said break from Marmaris. Bad timing though landing a bloke right before a holiday. Fuck I wish he was here with me… I have not let it stop me doing the tourist thing and have managed to go clothes shopping in Calpe and Moraira and even made it down to the beach to give my vampire skin a bit of colour.

Things are very much slower here than they are at home. Even though it's not my first time visiting I was still shocked to find that shops (including supermarkets) close from a Saturday afternoon right through to a Monday morning, during the week everyone has a siesta meaning that no shop in any town is open, and by the time I get up I have to wait another few hours before I can actually go shopping.
This is a very foreign feeling, good thing it's a holiday then isn't it.
I have however managed to keep to my usual routine of watching X Factor on Saturday and Sunday night. It's a good thing that my Mum likes watching it too as I could have really cramped their usual Saturday night dining out style... Ahh well, only child and all that :)

The olds have been dragging me around to each of their friends houses, I think they are showing me off. You see the last time I was here was for my Mums 60th birthday party three years ago and I suppose you could say that I made a bit of an arse of myself from getting wankered at her birthday bash. I refused to leave the party and although my parents had taken themselves off home, I stayed out drinking with their mates making a God holy show of myself.

So I believe that the olds wanted to prove to their pals that I am no longer a twat and more of a professional business woman now. Nope Mum, I'm still a twat but I will try to behave this holiday I swear.

We are heading down to Murcia on Thursday for an overnight break. Why? Primark's there, that's why. I have not been back to the UK for over a year and I generally go into spasms and palpitations if I haven't had a Primark visit in 6 months, and even though the one we are heading to is teeny tiny, I just don't care as I'm finally getting my Primark fix.
Go Spain!

Saffy has been giving me regular updates on Guch. I think she was surprised to find that he snores like a human and farts like one too. At least he seems to be having fun.

I have been informed by the dentist (we have been talking for hours) that it is freezing cold now in Marmaris. What the bloody fuck man, I am totally jealous as even though it started off grey here on Friday, it certainly isn't any more! Its shorts and t-shirt weather wouldn't you know it! Come on universe, give this sun stressed Minger a break and cloud over for just one sodding afternoon!

Back to the dentist; we have literally been talking nonstop. I really think that when I get back things are going to move in the right direction if the conversations we have been having are anything to go by… Honest to God, I really like him, and I get the feeling that he really likes me to. We had a discussion the other night about if during the one week break that we had, if either of us had 'shagged' with anyone else. Was he trying to let me know he had? I'm not 100% sure on that one, but he told me he hadn't. I won't bore you with all the chats but let me tell you, they have been quite serious to say the least… For Example: Going on holiday, moving in together, etc. Like I said, serioussssss!

Considering I was coming here to take a break from Marmaris and possibly find a bloke, I have done the exact opposite and bum off the one that I have left behind for two weeks. As they say, absence makes the heart grow fonder and it really has in the dentist's case. Anyway, back to the holiday: For once I have been rather snap happy with my camera. I haven't quite figured out how to actually get the correct date on the damn thing even though I have had the camera in my possession for 6 years. At the moment it is sitting on 2015. No matter what I do, it just won't change from that date, so I have given up.

I have not had much of a drink other than the odd Beer and G n T. This is what my Mother is calling my 'well overdue detox time'. It won't happen again for another 3.5 years, so I may as well make the most of it now.

Every time I announce that I am going outside for a fag I have to deal with the same old shit: the knowing looks and the '*one more nail in the coffin*' remarks every f'ing time. If they only knew that this makes me want to smoke more, if they could only see that when they tell me that I drink far too much it actually makes me want to open a bottle of vodka and polish the bugger off.
Parents eh, don't they know that if they only tried a bit of
reverse psychology on me that would work like a charm?

Ahh fuck it, its nearly time for 'Made in Chelsea', another TV staple that I get to keep whilst here.

Spain is not at all bad when visiting the olds. We haven't argued yet and I have been here for four days already!

27th Oct

Dear happy holiday maker,

I left my house two whole weeks ago tonight, on a mare of a journey, thinking I had all the time in the world before it had to be repeated. Alas, all the time in the world has arrived.

I have not drunk myself into oblivion much to my Mothers relief, yet I have not been allowed to stay in bed for the duration of the day either.

I have been too hot, too cold and just right. I have smoked less, drank less yet eaten more. I have spent up, not bought enough, yet am over weight with luggage.

What's a girl to do?

It's safe to say that I am going to have to go on one serious diet when I finally arrive home. Don't get me wrong, I have tried my hardest not to over eat, stuff my face, and in general, not to make too much of a pig out of myself. I have failed on all three counts.

Bang goes the outfit I was going to wear for Halloween. No such thing as a sexy cat that looks preggers. Have I had a good time filling my face with crap? Yes indeedie. I have eaten pizza and pasta and more pizza and British bread like it has been going out of fashion. Oh dear lord how I miss British bread in Marmaris. If they could just get one thing right, British bread should be it. I would ask for world peace; however there is more chance of the British bread so I have to go with the statistics.

There have been arguments (as I knew there would be eventually)...

While we were in Murcia and trying to locate Primark I could have killed myself. My Dad does not follow directions from the Sat Nav, or the road signs, or me when I could see Primark plain as day in the distance. This resulted in me having a hissy fit and my Dad almost turning around and heading home.

Could you imagine if I had come all this way and not had my Primark fix? There would have been a death in the family I kid you not...

There have also been laughs... My Dad decided that he was going to have 'patiently waiting' inscribed on his tomb stone after waiting an eternity for the Mother and I to get ready for dinners out.

I have had fun here to be sure; What with my Mum trying to do an impression of a French person and a French person overhearing it and taking great offence, Dad's comments telling my Mum to get her head out of the doughnut barrel, my Mums efforts to force feed me, and my full on hissy fits, Spain has been an absolute ball that is coming to a close for this year.
I wonder how long it will take me to get back next time? Not too long if Primark has anything to do with it.

I have not missed home as much as I thought. Usually when I come to Spain I really miss home. The last time I was with that bastard of an ex. God were we in love. I remember him asking me to get a flight back after just 4 days of being in Spain. I tell you if it wouldn't have broken my parent's hearts I would have done just that and jumped on the next flight. This time it was a bit different. I needed to get the hell out of Marmaris before I drove myself crazy. I needed the break and maybe I should have taken it earlier and for longer than two weeks, but hey, I got a holiday for once in a blue moon and time to reassess life. Have I actually reassessed life? No not really. All I have done is chat constantly with the dentist and imagine what our wedding is going to be like. OK, I may be getting a bit ahead of myself, but I swear, this really could be the final summer of vodka. This could actually be it. All the signs are there… All we do is laugh, he is as crazy as me and well sod it, the sex is fucking fantastic!

Things are indeed looking up! See, when you set a goal and stick to it, that goal can be met! My goal from the start of the season looks set to beeee! Now is it wrong to want a black wedding dress?

If I thought I was in for a quiet time when I get home, I would be mistaken. Chokri is leaving on Monday heading back to Tunisia so we are squeezing in one last X Factor night this Saturday, and after that has finished I am heading down to Bar Street to meet my dentist. The night may end with me a tad drunk slavering on my own shoulder. I don't intend to end in such a manner, but don't forget I have been off the pop for two whole weeks.
Then comes the Halloween party on Monday that the dentist has promised

he will attend with me and Team Minger.

Oh life is good right now and I am a happy Minger!

So, it's back to normality again soon. However, to get back to said normality I have to start my mare of a journey in the morning beginning with a two hour drive to Valencia airport.
Jesus.
I guess you will hear from me once again next millennium sometime?

Ciao for now! Shit, that's Italian isn't is.

Chapter 8 - The Winter Begins...

3rd November

Dear home sweet home…,

I got back from Spain on Saturday morning at 03.30am to an apartment that looked like a tramp had decided to go binning in it and rolled around in all the rubbish you could possibly image in the world. My house smelt of grotty knickers and there were nasty little flies all over the place.Bloody Saffy! I could have killed her for leaving the house in such a mess, but as I was so damn tired from my journey from hell, there was nothing left in me to attempt a cleanup of any description, so I decided to sod it, go to bed and deal with it in the morning. I didn't even obsess about the dentist before sleep even though I could have considering the phenomenal texts I got from him all the way from the airport until I arrived home. The thought of seeing him was just mind numbingly wild, however, tiredness took over and sleep won the battle...

When I woke up and after I had spent what seemed like an eternity cleaning, I made arrangements with the dentist to meet up with him later that night somewhere on Bar Street. And meet up we did. Actually we spent the whole of the weekend together including Sunday night when he stayed over again.

It seemed like progress was being made, it really did. That was until he decided he wasn't coming out for Halloween and I haven't seen him since.

Today is Thursday. In my mixed up mind I had thought that we were nearly a couple. How did I get it so ridiculously wrong? It's clear that I have managed to misread the signs once fucking more. Why? Well, it's like this: On Tuesday I asked him if he wanted to come over for dinner. He said he had to clean his house. Ok, fair enough. I didn't ask again if he wanted to hang out until today when we were chatting online. I asked if he wanted to do something tonight and he asked 'what exactly'. That was the first strike. Isn't hanging out together maybe with a DVD and a bit of heavy petting not enough? I asked if he had another idea as winter in Marmaris does not have much to offer. He said we would chat when he got home. So I waited. And waited. And waited.

Finally he asked me to go around to his house, but it was already 10pm. When I told him I was in my pjs, he told me to get dressed as he wanted to go to a gig starting at midnight. Maybe it's just me, but seriously, it was 10pm, I was feeling tired and he was being shitty because I said I had not washed my hair and that I didn't feel like going out. I know this guy is rather spontaneous, but come on, give a gal a bit of warning! If I had of washed my hair previous to this then it may have been different, however I am a gal that washes hair 2ce a week only and the hair was at its grossest stage. When I told him that I wasn't going to go, I stupidly thought he would then say "OK as you asked first, we can just hang out". But he didn't. I wished him a good evening to which he replied Thanks.

And that's how it is at this point in time.

Today he dropped a shit bomb. He informed me that he is going to Bangkok on holiday for 2/3 months and when he gets back he is going to move out of his apartment into somewhere *like* mine. Not mine you may note, somewhere *like* mine. Have I put him off or does he simply have no clue what he wants? A girl like me could get the wrong idea entirely. Let's face it; I did get the wrong idea entirely…

I am due on my period soon and feel a bit more emotional than usual; however, I am not happy with this situation.

Another shock, the bloody Player called me today. As I had deleted his number I didn't know who it was calling so I answered, having him catch me totally off guard. Apparently I had text him on Monday night when I got home from the Halloween party. How is beyond me as I don't have his number. But I have been known to find ways…

He asked if he could come over tonight to chat. Obviously I told him no as I thought I was on my way to playing happy couples. Now that I am drowning my sorrows in vodka, it seems like more of a good idea by the minute. And I do have his number again now…

What I really need to do is wait until the dentist has left his house and then send him an email telling him what I think of him. I need to curse and swear and sound like a crazy mad woman. After all, in one of his messages earlier, he asked me if I was on my period. Bastard was nearly right, but what woman wants to be asked that? I hate him, I really fucking hate him. I hate the fact that this shabby looking bloke has got under my skin and I have realised that I like him far too much for just casually seeing each other. And even though the tit asked about the holiday and moving in together, I now know he wasn't serious and that all this guy really wants is a piece of arse, and that is something that I am not. Well, not anymore anyway. I am a strong independent woman that will not be someone's second best. Why the hell should I? The only thing I am concerned about is that if I don't settle for his 2nd best, is there one really out there for me?

Come on dentist, man up. I do so like you.

8ᵗʰ November

Dear single wannabe socialite,

It's time to come to terms with the facts here diary. It's time to realize that I may be the unsavoury one in all of this seasons dating fiascos.

The dentist is over for good. He literally stopped replying to my calls, texts, MSNs and Facebook messages. He has not told me why so all I can assume is that he must have felt our thing had run its course. I shouldn't have been surprised as he told me right from the very. He was totally true to form. Well done him for sticking to his #Lifegoals!

After I had come to terms with this and a fair amount of stalking had been done, I found a post on bastard dentist's Facebook from one of his friends I hadn't met yet. The bloke was bloody cute too, just my type with his shaved head. So I added him to spite the dentist. I doubt he even knew that I did it, but it felt good anyway.

Cute bloke Barış and I started to chat online. Apparently he works in the rock bar that the dentist and I used to frequent and says we have spoken before. Well knock me down with a feather! He said he wondered who was the mysterious blonde clad in black and asked the dentist about me. What the dentist said shouldn't have come as a shock but it did. Apparently it seems that he had been trying to get rid of me for some time and had informed Barış that he could help set us up if he so wished. Fucking cunt. Seriously. I shall not waste any more time thinking about that mother fucker ever again. He must have felt such the big man that night. Bravo dentist, bravo!

Enough about him – I have arranged to meet up with Barış for coffee as he seems to be just what I'm looking for. Whether we click or whether we don't, I'm not obsessing. Well, not yet but give me time ;)

The Final Chapter

25th November

Dear the final summer of vodka,

The end is neigh. Or is it just the beginning? Either way, I do not have a ring on it.

I swear my life is like that 80's film 'The Never Ending ' but without the fluffy dragon that flies and instead the fluffy Guch that farts.

It's fair to say that this summer has seen some sights. Some that I wish never to see again, but all in all I think I have learnt some valuable lessons:

Lesson 1: I will never drink Absolute vodka again

Lesson 2: Love thy dog as he is the only man you can trust

Lesson 3: Whilst on diet tablets, be careful of farting as this can lead to follow through's of orange anal leakage

Lesson 4: Try not to argue with police men even if they are rude as

Lesson 5: I will not invite internet men to visit me for the weekend

Lesson 6: I will give the occasional someone the benefit of the doubt

I started the summer with one main goal: to find 'the one'. Have I found him? Have I shite. Over the course of this summer there have been hopefuls and not so hopefuls;

My kissing friend Kaan for example, he was a hopeful. He is a dear friend but I know that it can go no further as he is not going to leave his significant other. I am not a mistress, so we shall continue our friendship without the snogging. I know you were possibly rooting for this one diary, but no, it was not to be. Friendship means more than a grope on the sofa with an unobtainable buddy.

What about NLP guy? He was simply too shy for a gal like me and ended up being a total unhopeful. I need lightening, I need sparks. Did I get this with him? No. It also weirded me out that drinks redbull without vodka in it. That shit's just creepy.

The snappy dressing ex suitor; what started out as a possible hopeful turned into a farce. I have not seen or heard from him in quite some time, but as with all of these fuckers, they crawl out from under the woodwork when winter hits. And indeed winter has hit Marmaris. Sorry suitor, you're just too psycho for me what with asking for a key after 8 days of dating google translate.

The Yanki. Oh be Jesus that was just a sham from the start. I really liked the fact that he was American, spoke English, had a good brain and was a yacht captain at the young age of 27. I really didn't like the fact that he was overbearing, egotistical and opinionated. Thankfully he is no longer able to darken my doorstep in the hopes of a booty call as he has finally moved on to pastures new. I thank him for his efforts but not for losing my hip flask.

Big Dicky; A hopeful for another, just not for me. He is to be remembered by replacing my hip flask and having a limp dick. I really wish I could have liked this one; he would have been good for me. He was truly a nice fellow, flaccid cock and all.

What about the Player then? He keeps calling and texting. I no longer answer. After all, we have come full circle and there is simply no need to continue as it's going nowhere fast. I should have known that he would be a tit in a tin can, but quite frankly his looks floored me when he grew into the bad boy that I thought I wanted. He is Marmaris's own lothario and all he needs are a couple of tattoos and a Harley and by God he would make someone an excellent Colin Farrell. Although I do so love Colin, he turned out to be a total unhopeful.

The dreaded dentist -The eternally unhopeful: I really liked this one; alas it was not to be. I thought we had started something that looked like it could become serious, but his flaky personality put paid to that. He was not Mr Right, he was Mr Right Now. Although that was not on the agenda, we all have to live by the seat of our pants occasionally. I saw him in a club just a couple of days ago with a new female attached to his hip. He waved and raised his beer to say cheers then disappeared into the crowd. My stomach stayed firmly in place; there were no butterflies or anxiety from seeing him. In fact there was no feelings there at all. Maybe that's to do with dating his friend ;)

Although skinnier than what I usually go for, Bariş is courting me. Actually courting me. I am enjoying myself. I am not obsessing. He is giving me no reason to obsess and I'm not sure if that's a good or a bad thing. He loves Guch. That's an understatement, he actually adores Guch. I think Guch quite likes him too.

Bariş Status: Hopeful.

Whatever happens next is a mystery, a new adventure, an unfamiliar way forward. One thing I have learnt above anything else is not to live in the past, to never go back. So, with that in mind, that sodding ex that I was so in love with, the torrent of twats that have entered my life this summer will all stay where they are in the box labelled 'past' never to be reopened again.

To my great surprise I have enjoyed writing this diary. I may do it again one day. And Mum, if you have got this far without having a heart attack then fuck it, let's never speak of the written words again. If I see paragraphs circled then I am unfriending you on Facebook again.

And with that dear diary, I think it's time for a bloody big vodka and a snuggle up on the sofa with Gucci my one and only. I have a catch up planned with Team Minger tomorrow night so I need my beauty sleep.

So I bid you goodnight dear diary, goodnight and good luck to us all.

All my love,

Lei

Five Years Later...

04.05.16

Jesus I have read through my diary of 2011 and a whole load of memories came flooding back. Shit the bed I used to have an amazing social life didn't I? Ahh the dentist, how crazy obsessed I was and how I don't miss that feeling one little bit! A lot has happened in five years.

Some major points:

Major Point 1: Gucci is still my numero uno. That boy is a legend and my snuggle buddy. His farts are as vicious as ever and linger for friggin' days. If he could only speak he could write a book with his stories. It would be a best seller called 'Tales of me Mam'.

Major Point 2: I still drink vodka, as seriously, who the hell was I kidding thinking it was going to be my last summer of it?

Major Point 3: Team Minger is no more. Jess and I have sadly parted company. I remember our friendship fondly, however some friendships are not meant to last a lifetime. Kimmy, Sister and Kaan are still my closest pals ever and I see them all the time. There has been no snogging with Kaan since it was last documented here. He has not left his significant other.

Major Point 4: Oh, I'm bloody well married. But that is another that may also take another 5 years to consider getting down on paper / lap top ☺

Lots of love,

Lei

XXXXXXXX

ABOUT THE AUTHOR

Louise Bell lives in Marmaris, Turkey and has done since the sweet age of 16 years old. She is an ex rep, has a dog called Gucci and has certainly experienced her fair share of the single life. She is one of the more positive people that belong to this world and enjoys a glass of vodka from time to time, although red wine and diet coke is much more her favourable tipple.

Printed in Great Britain
by Amazon